Living Language™

CONVERSATIONAL
ITALIAN

THE LIVING LANGUAGE™ SERIES
BASIC COURSES ON CASSETTE
  *Spanish
  *French
  *German
  *Italian
  *Japanese
  *Portuguese (Continental)
  Portuguese (South American)
  Advanced Spanish
  Advanced French
  Children's Spanish
  Children's French
  Russian
  Hebrew
  English for Native Spanish Speakers
  English for Native French Speakers
  English for Native Italian Speakers
  English for Native German Speakers
  English for Native Chinese Speakers

*Also available on Compact Disc

LIVING LANGUAGE PLUS®
  Spanish
  French
  German
  Italian

LIVING LANGUAGE TRAVELTALK™
  Spanish
  French
  German
  Italian
  Russian

CONVERSATIONAL
ITALIAN

A COMPLETE COURSE
IN EVERYDAY ITALIAN

By Genevieve A. Martin

AND

Mario Ciatti

BASED ON THE METHOD DEVISED
BY RALPH WEIMAN FORMERLY CHIEF OF
LANGUAGE SECTION, U.S. WAR DEPARTMENT

SPECIALLY PREPARED FOR USE WITH
THE LIVING LANGUAGE COURSE IN ITALIAN

Crown Publishers, Inc., New York

This work was previously published under the title *Conversation Manual Italian*.

Copyright © 1956, 1985 by Crown Publishers, Inc.

THE LIVING LANGUAGE COURSE is a registered trademark, and CROWN, and LIVING LANGAGE and colophon are trademarks of Crown Publishers, Inc., 201 East 50th Street, New York, N.Y. 10022.

Library of Congress Catalog Card Number: 56-9317

ISBN 0-517-55790-8

1985 Updated Edition

Manufactured in the United States of America

18   17   16   15   14

TABLE OF CONTENTS

LETTER WRITING

INTRODUCTION to
the COMPLETE LIVING
LANGUAGE COURSE®

The Living Language Course® uses the natural method of language-learning. You learn Italian the way you learned English—by hearing the language and repeating what you heard. You didn't begin by studying grammar; you first learned how to say things, how words are arranged, and only when you knew the language pretty well did you begin to study grammar. This course teaches you Italian in the same way. Hear it, say it, absorb it through use and repetition. The only difference is that in this course the basic elements of the language have been carefully selected and condensed into 40 short lessons. When you have finished these lessons, you will have a good working knowledge of the language. If you apply yourself, you can master this course and learn to speak basic Italian in a few weeks.

While *Living Language™ Conversational Italian* is designed for use with the complete Living Language Course®, this book may be used without the cassettes. The first 5 lessons cover Italian pronunciation, laying the foundation for learning the vocabulary, phrases, and grammar that are explained in the later chapters.

All the material is presented in order of importance. When you reach page 150, you will have already learned 300 of the most frequently used sentences and will be able to make yourself understood on many important topics. By the time you have finished this course, you will have a sufficient command of Italian to get along in all ordinary situations.

The brief but complete summary of Italian grammar is included in the back of this book to enable you to perfect your knowledge of Italian. There are also many other helpful features, such as vocabulary tips, practice exercises, and verb charts. The special section on letter-writing will show you how to answer an invitation, make a business inquiry, and address an envelope properly. Just as important is the *Living Language*™ *Common Usage Dictionary*. This is included in the course primarily for use as a reference book, but it is a good idea to do as much browsing in it as possible. It contains the most common Italian words with their meanings illustrated by everyday sentences and idiomatic expressions. The basic words—those you should learn from the start—are capitalized to make them easy to find.

Keep practicing your Italian as much as possible. Once you are well along in the course, try reading Italian magazines, newspapers, and books. Use your Italian whenever you get a chance—with Italian-speaking friends, with the waiter at an Italian restaurant, with other students.

This course tries to make the learning of Italian as easy and enjoyable as possible, but a certain amount of application is necessary. The cassettes and books that make up this course provide you with all the material you need; the instructions on the next page tell you what to do. The rest is up to you.

Course Material

The material of the complete Living Language Course® consists of the following:

1. *2 hour-long cassettes*. The label on each face indicates clearly which lessons are contained on that side. (Living Italian is also available on 4 long-playing records.)

2. *Conversational Italian book*. This book is designed for use with the recorded lessons, or it may be used alone. It contains the following sections:
   Basic Italian Vocabulary and Grammar
   Summary of Italian Grammar
   Verb Charts
   Letter-writing

3. *Italian-English/English-Italian Common Usage Dictionary*. A special kind of dictionary that gives you the literal translations of more than 15,000 Italian words, plus idiomatic phrases and sentences illustrating the everyday use of the more important vocabulary and 1,000 essential words capitalized for ready reference.

How to Use Conversational Italian with the Living Language™ Cassettes

TO BEGIN
There are 2 cassettes with 10 lessons per side. The beginning of each lesson is announced on the tape and each lesson takes approximately 3 minutes. If your cassette player has a digit indicator, you can locate any desired point precisely.

LEARNING THE LESSONS

1. Look at page 1. Note the words in **boldface** type. These are the words you will hear on the cassette. There are pauses to enable you to repeat each word and phrase right after you hear it.

2. Now read Lesson 1. (The ▭ ▭ symbols indicate the beginning of the recorded material. In some advanced lessons, information and instructions precede the recording.) Note the points to listen for when you play the cassette. Look at the first word: **Alfredo**, and be prepared to follow the voice you will hear.

3. Play the cassette, listen carefully, and watch for the points mentioned. Then rewind, play the lesson again, and this time say the words aloud. Keep repeating until you are sure you know the lesson. The more times you listen and repeat, the longer you will remember the material.

4. Now go on to the next lesson. It's always good to quickly review the previous lesson before starting a new one.

5. There are 2 kinds of quizzes at the end of each section. One is the matching type, in which you must select the English translation of the Italian sentence. In the other, you fill in the blanks with the correct Italian word chosen from the 3 given directly below the sentence. Do these quizzes faithfully and, if you make any mistakes, reread the section.

6. When you get 100 percent on the Final Quiz, you may consider that you have mastered the course.

CONVERSATIONAL
ITALIAN

LESSON 1

1. THE LETTERS AND SOUNDS

(The Letters and Sounds I)

A. Many Italian sounds are similar to the English. Listen to and repeat the following Italian names, and notice which sounds are similar and which are different:

Alfredo	Alfred	**Luisa**	Louise
Antonio	Antonio	**Emmanuele**	Emanuel
Carlo	Charles	**Michele**	Michael
Caterina	Katherine	**Maria**	Mary
Enrico	Henry	**Pietro**	Peter
Elisabetta	Elizabeth	**Paolo**	Paul
Francesco	Francis	**Peppino**	Joe
Ferdinando	Ferdinand	**Raffaele**	Ralph
Isabella	Isabel	**Raimondo**	Raymond
Giovanni	John	**Rosa**	Rose
Giorgio	George	**Riccardo**	Richard
Giulia	Julia	**Roberto**	Robert
Guiseppe	Joseph	**Vincenzo**	Vincent
Luigi	Louis	**Violetta**	Violet

NOTICE:

1. that each vowel is pronounced clearly and crisply.

2. that a single consonant is pronounced with the following vowel.

3. that some vowels bear an accent mark, which sometimes shows the accentuated syllable:

la virtù   the virtue

but sometimes merely serves to distinguish words:

e   and   è   is

4. When the accent is on the letter *e*, it gives a more open pronunciation:

caffè   coffee

5. The apostrophe (') is used to mark the elision of a vowel.

B. Now listen to some geographical names:

Bari	**Napoli**
Brindisi	**Ravenna**
Genovoa	**Sardegna**
Livòrnò	**Sicilia**
Londra	**Taranto**
Messina	**Tevere**
Milano	**Venezia**

C. Now the names of some countries:

Argentina	**Inghilterra**
Belgio	**Messico**
Cina	**Norvegia**
Spagna	**Persia**
Stati Uniti	**Portogallo**
India	**Egitto**
Francia	**Venezuela**
Germania	**Russia**

LESSON 2

(The Letters and Sounds II)

D. Now listen to and repeat the following words which are similar in English and Italian. Notice how Italian spelling and pronunciation differ from English:

azione	action	**nazione**	nation
agente	agent	**necessario**	necessary
attenzione	attention	**posibile**	possible
caso	case	**quieto**	quiet
centro	center	**radio**	radio
certo	certain	**ristorante**	restaurant
differente	different	**simile**	similar
difficile	difficult	**tè**	tea
esempio	example	**teatro**	theater
gala	gala	**telefono**	telephone
chitarra	guitar	**treno**	train
importante	important	**visita**	visit
interessante	interesting		

2. THE ITALIAN ALPHABET

Letter	Name	Letter	Name	Letter	Name
a	a	h	acca	q	qu
b	bi	i	i	r	erre
c	ci	l	elle	s	esse
d	di	m	emme	t	ti
e	e	n	enne	u	u
f	effe	o	o	v	vi
g	gi	p	pi	z	zeta

LESSON 3

3. PRONUNCIATION PRACTICE

(Pronunciation Practice I)

The following groups of words will give you some additional practice in Italian pronunciation and spelling:

attore	actor	**umore**	humor
animale	animal	**locale**	local
capitale	capital	**materiale**	material
centrale	central	**originale**	original
cereale	cereal	**personale**	personal
cioccolato	chocolate	**probabile**	probable
colore	color	**regolare**	regular
dottore	doctor	**simile**	similar
familiare	familiar	**semplice**	simple
gas	gas	**totale**	total
generale	general	**usuale**	usual

A. VOWELS

1. *a* is like *ah*, or the *a* in *father*:

a	to, at	**lago**	lake
amico	friend	**pane**	bread
la	the *(fem. sing.)*		
		parlare	to speak

2. *e* is like the *ay* in *day,* but cut off sharply (that is, not drawled):

era	was	**treno**	train
essere	to be	**tre**	three
pera	pear	**estate**	summer
padre	father	**se**	if
carne	meat		

    e in the middle of a word may have two different sounds when stressed:

a. open sound:		b. closed sound:	
petto	chest	**verde**	green
terra	earth		

Some words even have different meanings according to whether the vowel has an open or closed sound:

(open)	**tema**	composition	(closed)	**tema**	fear
	venti	winds		**venti**	twenty

3. *i* is like the *i* in *police*, *machine*, *marine*, but not drawled:

misura	measure	**oggi**	today
si	yes	**piccolo**	small *(masc. sing.)*
amica	friend *(fem.)*	**figlio**	son

4. *o* is like the *o* in *no*, but not drawled:

no	no	**con**	with
poi	then	**otto**	eight
ora	hour	**come**	how

o in the middle of a word may have two different sounds when stressed:

a. open sound:		b. closed sound:	
oro	gold	**forma**	form
corpo	body	**voce**	voice

5. *u* is like the *u* in *rule*, but not drawled:

uno	one *(masc.)*	**tu**	you *(familiar)*
una	one *(fem.)*	**ultimo**	last

6. Notice that each vowel is clearly pronounced. Vowels are not slurred as they often are in English:

Europa	Europe	**poesia**	poem
leggere	to read	**creare**	to create
dov' è	where is	**mio**	my
io sono	I am	**paese**	country
idea	idea		

B. DIPHTHONGS

1. *ai:*
   guai troubles
2. *au:*
   aula room   *auto* auto   *aurora* dawn
3. *ei:*
   sei six   *seicento* six hundred
4. *eu:*
   Europa Europe
5. *ia:*
   Italia Italy   *patria* country   *aria* air
6. *ie:*
   piede foot   *bietola* beet   *tieni* (you) keep
7. *io:*
   stazione station   *fiore* flower   *piove* it is
                                    raining
8. *iu:*
   fiume river   *piuma* feather
9. *oi:*
   poi then   *voi* you
10. *ua:*
    quale what   *quattro* four   *quanto* how much
11. *ue:*
    questo this   *quello* that
12. *ui:*
    fui (I) was   *lui* him
13. *uo:*
    buono good   *tuo* your *(familiar)*

C. TRIPHTHONGS

1. *iei:*
   miei my (pronounce: yeh - ee)
2. *iuo:*
   figliuolo son (pronounce: you - oh)
3. *uoi:*
   tuoi your *(familiar)* (pronounce: woe - ee)

LESSON 4

A. CONSONANTS

(Pronunciation Practice II)

1. *b* is pronounced like the English *b* in *boat*:

bottiglia   bottle

2. *c* has two different sounds; before *a, o, u,* it is equivalent to the English *k* in *bake*:

caso   case

before *e* or *i* it is equivalent to the English *ch* in *church*:

celibe   bachelor

3. *d* is like the English *d* in *dark*:

data   date

4. *f* is also equivalent to the corresponding English letter:

forza   force

5. *g* has two different sounds: before *a, o, u,* it is equivalent to the English *g* in *go*:

guida   guide

before *e* or *i,* it is equivalent to the English *g* in *general*:

generoso   generous

6. *h* is not pronounced. It is found only in exclamations:

ah!   ah!

or in certain forms of the verb to have:

io ho   I have

7. *l, m, n, p,* are equivalent to the corresponding letters in English:

libertà	liberty	**notte**	night
memoria	memory	**prova**	proof

8. *q* is only in combination with *u* and is pronounced like the English *qu* in *quality.*

quarto	quarter

9. *r* is more rolled than in English, somewhat as in Scotch pronounciation:

regione	region

10. *s* has two different sounds:
  a. harsh at the beginning of a word, or when used double, or preceded by another consonant:

sale	salt	**console**	consul
rosso	red		

  b. soft when occurring between two vowels:

causa	cause	**poesia**	poetry
esilio	exile		

11. *t, v,* are equivalent to the corresponding letters in English:

tono	tone	**vacanza**	vacation

12. *z* has two different sounds:
  a. harsh, as in the English combination *ts.* This sound generally occurs in the group *-zione.*

azione	action	**addizione**	addition
nazione	nation		

b. soft, as in the English combination *ds*. This sound occurs mostly in technical and classical words derived from Greek.

zona	zone	**azoto**	azote
zeffiro	zephyr		

B. SPECIAL ITALIAN SOUNDS

Pay special attention to the following sounds, which do not have exact English equivalents:

1. *cc* when followed by *i* or *e* is pronounced like the English *ch* in *chair*:

cacciatore	hunter	**faccia**	face

2. *ch* before *e* and *i* is pronounced like the English *k* in *key*:

chitarra	guitar	**chiodo**	nail

3. *gh* before *e* and *i* is pronounced like the English *g* in *gate*:

ghirlanda	garland	**ghermire**	(to) clutch

4. *gli* is a sound found only in Italian; the closest English approximation would be the combination *lli*, as in *million*:

egli	he	**paglia**	straw
foglia	leaf	**giglio**	lily

5. *gn* is always pronounced as one letter, somewhat like the English *ni* in *onion*, or *ny* in *canyon*:

segno	sign	**Spagna**	Spain
montagna	mountain	**lavagna**	blackboard

6. *sc* before *e* and *i* is pronounced like the English *sh* in *shoe*:

scendere	(to) climb	**sciroppo**	syrup
scimmia	monkey	**scivolare**	(to) slip

7. *sc* before *a, o,* and *u,* is pronounced like the English *sk* in *sky*:

scuola	school	**Scozia**	Scotland
scarpa	shoe	**scoiattolo**	squirrel

4. BUILDING UP A VOCABULARY

Building up an Italian vocabulary is a rather easy matter since a great number of words are similar in English and Italian. Some words are spelled exactly the same (though they may differ considerably in pronunciation):

Italian	English	Italian	English
antenna	antenna	*velocipede*	velocipede
area	area	*idea*	idea
auto	auto	*gas*	gas
radio	radio	*hotel*	hotel

There are many Italian words which you will have no difficulty in recognizing despite minor differences. Some of these differences are:

a. The Italian words add *e*

annuale	annual	*parte*	part
commerciale	commercial	*origine*	origin
occasionale	occasional	*speciale*	special
professionale	professional		

b. The Italian words add *a* or *o*

lista	list	*costo*	cost
problema	problem	*liquido*	liquid
persona	person		

c. The Italian words have *a* or *o* where the English ones have *e*

causa	cause	*favorito*	favorite
figura	figure	*minuto*	minute
medicina	medicine	*tubo*	tube
rosa	rose	*uso*	use

5. GENERAL EQUIVALENTS

1. Italian *c (cc)* = English *k (ck)*:

franco	frank	*parco*	park
sacco	sack	*attacco*	attack

2. Italian *f* = English *ph*:

frase	phrase	*telegrafo*	telegraph
fisico	physical	*fonico*	phonic

3. Italian *s (ss)* = English *x*:

esercizio	exercise	*Messico*	Mexico
esempio	example	*fisso*	fix

4. Italian *st* = English *xt*:

estensione	extension	*estremo*	extreme
estorto	extorted		

5. Italian *t* = English *th*:

autore	author	*teatro*	theatre
simpatia	sympathy	*teoria*	theory

6. Italian *z (zz)* = English *c*:

forza	force	*razza*	race

7. Italian *i* = English *y*:

stile	style	*sistema*	system
mistero	mystery	*ritmo*	rhythm

8. Italian *o* = English *ou*:

corte	court	*corso*	course
monte	mount		

9. Italian *-io* = English *-y*:

segretario	secretary	*territorio*	territory

10. Italian *-zione* = English *-tion*:

nazione	nation	*addizione*	addition
conversazione	conversation		

11. Italian *-o* = English *-al*:

interno	internal	*politico*	political
eterno	eternal		

12. Italian *-oso* = English *-ous*:

famoso	famous	*prodigioso*	prodigious
numeroso	numerous	*religioso*	religious

LESSON 5

6. USEFUL WORD GROUPS

(Useful Word Groups)

SOME NUMBERS

uno	one
due	two
tre	three
quattro	four
cinque	five
sei	six

sette	seven
otto	eight
nove	nine
dieci	ten

THE DAYS OF THE WEEK[1]

lunedì	Monday
martedì	Tuesday
mercoledì	Wednesday
giovedì	Thursday
venerdì	Friday
sabato	Saturday
domenica	Sunday

THE MONTHS

gennaio	January
febbraio	February
marzo	March
aprile	April
maggio	May
giugno	June
luglio	July
agosto	August
settembre	September
ottobre	October
novembre	November
dicembre	December

SOME COLORS

rosso	red
blu	blue
verde	green
nero	black
bianco	white

[1]The names of the days of the week and of the months are never capitalized.

giallo	yellow
marrone	brown (coffee-color)
castagno	brown (chestnut-color)
grigio	gray

THE SEASONS

primavera	spring
estate	summer
autunno	autumn
inverno	winter

NORTH, SOUTH, EAST, WEST

nord	north
sud	south
est	east
ovest	west

MORNING, NOON, AND NIGHT

mattina	morning
mezzogiorno	noon
pomeriggio	afternoon
sera	evening
notte	night

TODAY, YESTERDAY, TOMORROW

oggi	today
ieri	yesterday
domani	tomorrow

Oggi è venerdì.	Today is Friday.
Ieri esta giovedì.	Yesterday was Thursday.
Domani è sabato.	Tomorrow is Saturday.

Uno più uno fa due.	One and one are two.
Uno più due fa tre.	One and two are three.
Due più due fanno quattro.	Two and two are four.

Due più tre fanno cinque.	Two and three are five.
Tre più tre fanno sei.	Three and three are six.
Tre più quattro fanno sette.	Three and four are seven.
Quattro più quattro fanno otto.	Four and four are eight.
Cinque più quattro fanno nove.	Five and four are nine.
Cinque più cinque fanno dieci.	Five and five are ten.

QUIZ 1

Try matching these two columns:

1.	*venerdì*	1.	January
2.	*autunno*	2.	summer
3.	*giovedì*	3.	June
4.	*primavera*	4.	winter
5.	*otto*	5.	October
6.	*gennaio*	6.	white
7.	*inverno*	7.	autumn
8.	*verde*	8.	Sunday
9.	*giugno*	9.	eight
10.	*estate*	10.	spring
11.	*lunedì*	11.	west
12.	*quattro*	12.	Thursday
13.	*ottobre*	13.	four
14.	*domenica*	14.	ten
15.	*ovest*	15.	red
16.	*rosso*	16.	black
17.	*nero*	17.	green
18.	*dieci*	18.	Friday
19.	*bianco*	19.	gray
20.	*grigio*	20.	Monday

ANSWERS

1-18; 2-7; 3-12; 4-10; 5-9; 6-1; 7-4; 8-17; 9-3; 10-2;
11-20; 12-13; 13-5; 14-8; 15-11; 16-15; 17-16;
18-14; 19-6; 20-19.

LESSON 6

7. GOOD MORNING!

(Useful Phrases I)

NELLA MATTINA:	IN THE MORNING:
buon	good
giorno	morning (day)
Buon giorno.	Good morning.
signor	Mr.
Rossi	Rossi
Buon giorno, signor Rossi.	Good morning, Mr. Rossi.
come	how
sta	are you
Come sta?	How are you? How do you do?
molto	very
bene	well
Molto bene.	Very well.
grazie	thank you, thanks
Molto bene, grazie.	Very well, thank you.
E lei?	And how are you? (And you?)[1]
bene	fine
Bene, grazie.	Fine, thank you.

[1]Words in parentheses are literal translations.

NELLA SERA:	IN THE AFTERNOON:
buona	good
sera	afternoon
Buona sera.	Good afternoon.
Buona sera, signora Rossi.	Good afternoon, Mrs. Rossi.
Buona notte.	Good night.
Buona notte, signor Rossi.	Good night, Mr. Rossi.

Note: The Italian word for "sir" or "Mr." is *signore,* but when it is used immediately preceding a name, the *e* is dropped.

Buon giorno, signor Rossi.
Buon giorno, signore.

QUIZ 2

1.	*mattina*	1.	Good afternoon.
2.	*signora*	2.	How are you?
3.	*E lei?*	3.	Miss
4.	*molto bene*	4.	morning
5.	*Buon giorno.*	5.	Thank you.
6.	*Buona notte.*	6.	Madam or Mrs.
7.	*Come sta?*	7.	nothing new
8.	*oggi*	8.	sir or Mr.
9.	*Grazie.*	9.	How?
10.	*nulla de nuovo*	10.	Good morning.
11.	*signorina*	11.	in the afternoon
12.	*Buona sera.*	12.	And you?
13.	*Come?*	13.	very well
14.	*signore*	14.	today
15.	*di sera*	15.	Good evening (good night).

ANSWERS

1-4; 2-6; 3-12; 4-13; 5-10; 6-15; 7-2; 8-14; 9-5;
10-7; 11-3; 12-1; 13-9; 14-8; 15-11.

8. WHERE IS...?

dove	where
è	is
dov'è	where is
Dov'è un albergo? (hotel)	Where is a hotel?
buon ristorante	good restaurant
Dov'è un buon ristorante?	Where's a good restaurant?
dov'è (dove è)	where is
Dov'è?	Where is it?
Dov'è il telefono?	Where's the telephone?
Dov'è il ristorante?	Where's the restaurant?
Dov'è la stazione ferroviaria?	Where's the railroad station?
Dov'è l'ufficio postale?	Where's the post office?

LESSON 7

(Useful Phrases II)

può dirmi lei	can you tell me
Può dirmi lei...?	Can you tell me...?
Può dirmi lei dov'è un albergo?	Can you tell me where is a hotel?
Può dirmi lei dov'è un buon ristorante?	Can you tell me where is a good restaurant?
Può dirmi dov'è il telefono?	Can you tell where the telephone is?
Può dirmi dov'è la stazione ferroviaria?	Can you tell me where the station is?
Può dirmi dov'è l'ufficio postale?	Can you tell me where the post office is?

QUIZ 3

1. *Dov'è un albergo?*	1. Where's the telephone?
2. *Dov'è il telefono?*	2. Can you tell me where the station is?
3. *Può dirmi lei . . . ?*	3. Can you tell me . . . ?
4. *Può dirmi dov'è la stazione ferroviaria?*	4. the post office
5. *l'ufficio postale*	5. Where's there a hotel?

ANSWERS

1-5; 2-1; 3-3; 4-2; 5-4.

9. DO YOU HAVE . . . ?

Ha lei . . . ?	Do you have . . . ?
denaro	(any) money
sigarette	(any) cigarettes
fiammiferi	(any) matches
Ho bisogno di . . .	I need . . .
carta	(some) paper
matita	a pencil
inchiostro	ink
un francobollo	a stamp
pasta dentifricia	toothpaste
un asciugamano	a towel
Dove posso comprare . . . ?	Where can I buy . . . ?
un dizionario italiano	an Italian dictionary
un dizionario inglese-italiano	an English-Italian dictionary
un libro in inglese	an English book
degli abiti	some clothes

10. WHAT DO YOU HAVE TO EAT?

prima colazione	breakfast
seconda colazione	lunch
pranzo	dinner
cena	supper
Che cosa desidera?	What will you have? (What do you wish?)
Mi dia la lista, per favore.	Give me the menu, please.
Posso avere la lista, per favore?	May I have a menu, please?
Mi porti . . .	Bring me . . .
un po' di pane	some bread
pane e burro	bread and butter
della minestra	some soup
della carne	some meat
del manzo	some beef
una bistecca	a steak
del prosciutto	some ham
del pesce	some fish
del pollo	some chicken
delle uova	some eggs
dei legumi	some vegetables
delle patate	some potatoes
dell'insalata	some salad
dell'acqua	some water
del vino	some wine
della birra	some beer
del latte	some milk
caffè e latte	coffee with milk
dello zucchero	some sugar
del sale	some salt
del pepe	some pepper
della frutta	some fruit
dei dolci	some dessert

Mi porti . . .	Bring me . . .
una tazza di caffè	a cup of coffee
una tazza di tè	a cup of tea
un tovagliolo	a napkin
un cucchiaio	a spoon
un cucchiaino	a teaspoon
un coltello	a knife
un piatto	a plate
un bicchiere	a glass

Desidero . . .	I would like . . .
un po' di frutta	some fruit (assorted)
una bottiglia di vino	a bottle of wine
un' altra bottiglia di vino	another bottle of wine
un po' di più	a little more
un po' più di pane	a little more bread
un po' più di carne	a little more meat
Il conto, per favore.	The check, please

QUIZ 4

1.	*carne*	1.	fish
2.	*patate*	2.	water
3.	*acqua*	3.	vegetables
4.	*Che cosa desidera?*	4.	I need soap.
5.	*uova*	5.	The check, please.
6.	*pollo*	6.	breakfast
7.	*pesce*	7.	a spoon
8.	*una bottiglia di vino*	8.	coffee with milk
9.	*Ho bisogno di sapone.*	9.	What will you have?
10.	*Mi dia un po' di pane.*	10.	dessert
11.	*caffè e latte*	11.	meat

12.	*zucchero*	12.	a knife
13.	*legumi*	13.	eggs
14.	*una tazza di tè*	14.	Bring me some bread.
15.	*un po' più di pane*	15.	chicken
16.	*un coltello*	16.	a cup of tea
17.	*dolci*	17.	a little more bread
18.	*colazione*	18.	sugar
19.	*un cucchiaio*	19.	a bottle of wine
20.	*Il conto, per favore.*	20.	potatoes

ANSWERS

1-11; 2-20; 3-2; 4-9; 5-13; 6-15; 7-1; 8-19; 9-4; 10-14; 11-8; 12-18; 13-3; 14-16; 15-17; 16-12; 17-10; 18-6; 19-7; 20-5.

LESSON 8

11. SOME COMMON VERB FORMS

(Some Common Verb Forms)

io parlo	I speak
tu parli	you speak *(familiar)*
egli parla	he speaks
ella parla	she speaks
lei parla	you speak *(polite)*
noi parliamo	we speak
voi parlate	you speak *(plural or formal)*
essi parlano	they speak *(masc.)*
esse parlano	they speak *(fem.)*
loro parlano	you speak *(polite)* or they speak

NOTES

1. These forms, which make up the present tense of the first conjugation, are also commonly used to translate the English "I am speaking" and "I do speak."

2. *Tu,* you, is used to address people you know very well (whom you call by their first names in English—relatives, close friends, children, pets, etc.) The plural for *tu* is *voi. Voi* is also used to address one or more persons as an intermediate form between the intimate *tu* and the formal *lei.*

3. Notice that there are six endings which indicate the person speaking or spoken about, without need of pronoun:

   Singular:

—o	indicates the speaker (I)
—i	indicates the person spoken to (you). It is used only to someone or something you know well.
—a	indicates someone or something spoken about (he, she, it) or else you *(polite).*

   Plural:

—iamo	indicates several speakers (we).
—ate	is the plural form for *tu. Voi* is also used to address one or more persons in a formal way.
—ano	indicates they (both masculine and feminine) or the plural of the polite form.

4. Notice that the verb form with *lei, egli, ella* is the same: *parla.*

5. Notice that several forms of the pronouns differ, depending on whether men or women are speaking or are being spoken about:

egli parla	he is speaking
ella parla	she is speaking
essi parlano	they are speaking (men)
esse parlano	they are speaking (women)

6. *Lei, loro, le, la, li* (you) are sometimes capitalized to emphasize the idea of respect toward a person—for instance, when writing a formal letter or addressing someone in a respectful way.

12. THE and A

1. The

masculine

il libro	the book	*i libri*	the books
lo studio	the study	*gli studi*	the studies
l'esercizio	the exercise	*gli esercizi*	the exercises

feminine

la donna	the lady	*le donne*	the ladies
l'erba	the grass	*le erbe*	the grass, grasses

Notice the different forms used in Italian for the single English word "the." In Italian, words are either masculine or feminine. When they refer to males or females, you know which group of articles to use, but in the case of other nouns, you have to learn whether the noun is masculine or feminine. The masculine article *il* and its plural form *i* is used before masculine nouns beginning with a consonant. The masculine article *lo* and it plural form *gli* is used before masculine nouns beginning with a vowel or a *z*, or *s* plus a consonant, or the consonant combination *gn*. When used before a vowel, *lo* is elided to *l'*; the plural does not elide unless the following word begins with an *i*. The feminine article *la* and its plural form *le* is used before feminine nouns; however, before vowels, it is also elided to *l'* especially u- in the singular.

2. A (An)

un ragazzo	a boy	*una ragazza*	a girl
uno zero	a zero	*un'amica*	a friend *(fem.)*

The indefinite article has the form *un* before vowels and most consonants. It takes the form *uno* before the consonant *z*, or *s* plus a consonant, or the combination *gn*. The feminine is *una,* eliding to *un'* before a vowel.

QUIZ 5

1.	*io*	1.	they speak
2.	*noi*	2.	she is speaking
3.	*tu parli*	3.	she
4.	*egli*	4.	you *(fam. plur.)*
5.	*essi parlano*	5.	I
6.	*voi*	6.	you speak
7.	*tu*	7.	he
8.	*ella*	8.	we speak
9.	*noi parliamo*	9.	you *(fam. sing.)*
10.	*ella parla*	10.	we

ANSWERS
1-5; 2-10; 3-6; 4-7; 5-1; 6-4; 7-9; 8-3; 9-8; 10-2.

13. SOME COMMON CONTRACTIONS

di + il = del (of the)	*a + il = al* (to the)
di + lo = dello	*a + lo = allo*
di + la = della	*a + la = alla*
di + l' = dell'	*a + l' = all'*
di + i = dei	*a + i = ai*
di + gli = degli	*a + gli = agli*
di + le = delle	*a + le = alle*
con + il = col (with the)	*su + il = sul* (on the)
con + i = coi	*su + la = sulla*
	su + lo = sullo
	su + gli = sugli

14. PLURAL OF NOUNS

As a general rule, nouns ending in *o* are masculine.

As a general rule, nouns ending in *a* are feminine.

As a general rule, nouns ending in *e* can be either masculine or feminine.

All masculine nouns (ending either in *o* or *e*) form their plural in *i*.

All feminine nouns form their plural in *e* or *i* depending on whether they end in *a* or *e* in the singular.

il piatto	the plate	*i piatti*	the plates
il cuore	the heart	*i cuori*	the hearts
la rosa	the rose	*le rose*	the roses
la valle	the valley	*le valli*	the valleys

15. ADJECTIVES

There are two groups of adjectives:

1. Those which have four endings:

   caro (masc. sing.), cara (fem. sing.)
   cari (masc. plur.), care (fem. plur.)

2. Those which have only two endings:
   gentile (masc. and fem. sing.)
   gentili (masc. and fem. plur.)

Study these examples:

un caro amico	a dear friend *(masc.)*
una cara amica	a dear friend *(fem.)*
dei cari amici	some dear friends *(masc.)*
delle care amiche	some dear friends *(fem.)*
un uomo gentile	a kind man *(masc.)*
una donna gentile	a kind woman *(fem.)*
degli uomini gentili	some kind men *(masc.)*
delle donne gentili	some kind women *(fem.)*

The adjective always agrees with its noun. When an adjective is used alone, its ending usually tells you whether it refers to a singular or plural, feminine or masculine noun:

È italiano.	He is Italian.
È italiana.	She is Italian.
Sono italiani.	They are Italian *(masc.)*
Sono italiane.	They are Italian *(fem.)*

Note: Only proper names and geographical nouns are capitalized in Italian. Names of nationalities are capitalized only when used as nouns and referring to a person. When used as adjectives, or to refer to a language, they are not capitalized.

Examples:

un libro italiano	an Italian book
Ho incontrato un Italiano.	I met an Italian.
Essi parlano l'italiano.	They speak Italian.

16. POSSESSION

English – *'s* or – *s'* is translated by *di* (of):

il libro di Giovanni	John's book (the book of John)
i libri dei ragazzi	the boys' books (the books of the boys)

17. ASKING A QUESTION

To ask a question you can either put the subject after the verb:

Ha mangiato lei?	Have you eaten?

or preserve the same word order and raise your voice at the end of the sentence to show that it is a question:

Lei ha mangiato.	You have eaten.
Lei ha mangiato?	Have you eaten?

18. NOT

The word for "not" is *non*. It come before the verb.

Non vedo	I don't see

REVIEW QUIZ 1

1. *Buon* _____ (morning), *signora Rossi.*
   a. *domani*
   b. *giorno*
   c. *grazie*

2. *Può dirmi* _____ (where's) *l'ufficio postale?*
   a. *dov'è*
   b. *buono*
   c. *lì*

3. _____ (Bring me) *un po' di pane.*
   a. *Mangiare*
   b. *Sera*
   c. *Mi porti*

4. *caffè con* _____ (milk)
   a. *zucchero*
   b. *vino*
   c. *latte*

5. *un po'* _____ (more) *di carne*
   a. *più*
   b. *tazza*
   c. *ancora*

6. *il sette* _____ (January)
   a. *marzo*
   b. *gennaio*
   c. *agosto*

7. _____ (Wednesday), *cinque settembre*
   a. *inverno*
   b. *sabato*
   c. *mercoledì*

8. _____ (How) *sta?*
   a. *Grazie*
   b. *Come*
   c. *Sera*

9. *Buona* _____ (night), *signorina Rossi.*
   a. *fino*
   b. *notte*
   c. *io*

10. *Desidero una bottiglia di* _____ (wine).
    a. *latte*
    b. *vino*
    c. *àcqua*

ANSWERS

1-b; 2-a; 3-c; 4-c; 5-a; 6-b; 7-c; 8-b; 9-b; 10-b.

19. MAY I INTRODUCE . . . ?

Buon giorno.	Good morning.
Buon giorno, signore.	Good morning, (sir).
Come sta?	How are you?
Molto bene, grazie, e come sta lei? È lei americano?	Very well, thanks, and how are you? Are you from the United States?
Sì, signore.	Yes, (sir).
Parla lei italiano?	Do you speak Italian?
Un poco.	A little.
La presento alla mia amica signorina Rossi.	I present you to my friend Miss Rossi.
Posso presentarle la mia amica, signorina Rossi?	May I introduce my friend, Miss Rossi?

Molto piacere di conoscerla.	Much pleasure in knowing you.
Felice di conoscerla.	I'm glad (happy) to know you.
Il piacere è mio.	The pleasure is mine.
Mi permetta che mi presenti: Giovanni Rossi.	Permit me to introduce myself: John Rossi.
Mi permetta che mi presenti? Sono Giovanni Rossi.	May I introduce myself? I am John Rossi.
Paolo Ferri.	Paul Ferri.
Sono Paolo Ferri.	I'm Paul Ferri.

20. IT'S BEEN A REAL PLEASURE

È stato un vero piacere.	It's been a real pleasure.
È stato un vero piacere.	It's been a real pleasure.
Il piacere è stato mio.	The pleasure has been mine.
Il piacere è stato mio.	The pleasure was mine.
Arrivederci ad un altro giorno.	Good-by until another day.
A presto.	See you soon.
Arrivederci. A presto.	Good-by. See you soon.
a più tardi	until later
A più tardi.	Until later. See you soon.
Buona notte.	Good night.

LESSON 9

21. HOW ARE THINGS?

(Simple Sentences I)

Buon giorno, Paolo!	Hello, Paul!
Buon giorno, Giovanni!	Hello, John!
Come stai? Come vanno le cose?	How are you? *(familiar)* How are things?
Bene, e tu?	Fine, and how are you?
che	what
c'è	is there
di nuovo	of new
Che c'è di nuovo?	What's new?
nulla	nothing
di	of
particolare	particular
Nulla di particolare.	Nothing in particular.
che	what
mi racconti	do (you) tell me
Che mi racconti?	What's new?
poche	little
cose	things
Non molto.	Not much.

QUIZ 6

1. *Come stai?*	1. Nothing in particular.
2. *Arrivederci.*	2. Allow me to introduce my friend.
3. *Buona notte.*	3. See you soon.
4. *Buon giorno, Giovanni.*	4. Hello, John.
5. *Nulla di particolare.*	5. I'm very glad to know you.

6. *Mi permetta di presentarla al mio amico.*

7. *A presto*
8. *nuovo*
9. *Molto piacere di conoscerla.*
10. *conoscerla*

6. How are you?

7. Good night.
8. to know you
9. new

10. So long.

ANSWERS
1-6; 2-10; 3-7; 4-4; 5-1; 6-2; 7-3; 8-9; 9-5; 10-8.

22. TO BE

io sono	I am
tu sei	you are
egli è	he is
noi siamo	we are
vio siete	you are
essi sono	they are

Egli è dottore.	He is a doctor.
Egli è scrittore.	He is a writer.
Egli è italiano.	He's an Italian.

Il libro è rosso.	The book is red.
Ella è giovane.	She is young.
Il ghiaccio è freddo.	Ice is cold.
Egli è intelligente.	He's intelligent.
Ella è incantevole.	She's charming.

Sono io.	It's I.

Di dov'è lei?	Where are you from?
Io sono italiano.	I'm Italian.
È fatto di legno.	It's made of wood.
È d'argento.	It's silver.

Di chi è questo?	Whose is this?
Il libro è del signor Rossi.	The book belongs to Mr. Rossi.

È l'una.	It's one o'clock.
Sono le due.	It's two o'clock.
Sono le nove e dieci.	It's ten past nine.

Sono a quindici soldi la dozzina.	They are fifteen cents a dozen.
Sono nove dollari l'uno.	They are nine dollars each.

È tardi.	It's late.
È presto.	It's early.
È necessario.	It's necessary.
È un peccato.	It's a pity.
Non è vero?	Isn't it?

QUIZ 7

1. *Egli è intelligente.*	1. Whose is this?
2. *È ub peccato. Peccato.*	2. Where are you from?
3. *Egli è dottore.*	3. They are.
4. *Io sono.*	4. He's a doctor.
5. *È l'una.*	5. It's early.
6. *Noi siamo.*	6. He's Italian.
7. *È fatto di legno.*	7. He's intelligent.
8. *Di dov'è lei?*	8. It's a pity. Too bad.
9. *È presto.*	9. I am.

10. *Io sono stanco.*	10. It's one o'clock.
11. *Essi sono.*	11. It's made of wood.
12. *Di chi è questo?*	12. We are.
13. *È tardi.*	13. I'm tired.
14. *Egli è italiano.*	14. It's late.

ANSWERS

1-7; 2-8; 3-4; 4-9; 5-10; 6-12; 7-11; 8-2; 9-5; 10-13;
11-3; 12-1; 13-14; 14-6.

23. IT IS

È . . .	It is . . .
È vero	It's true.
Questo non è vero.	That isn't true.
Questo non è così.	That isn't so.
È così. Così è.	It's so. That's the way it is.
È male.	It's bad.
È molto male.	It's very bad.
È certo.	It's certain.
È grande.	It's big.
È piccolo.	It's small.
È caro.	It's expensive.
È economico.	It's cheap.
È vicino.	It's near.
È lontano.	It's far.
È difficile.	It's difficult.
È facile.	It's easy.
È poco. Non è molto.	It's a little. It's not much.
È molto poco.	It's very little.
È molto.	It's a lot.
È abbastanza.	It's enough.
Non è abbastanza.	It's not enough.
È qui.	It's here.

È lì.	It's there.
È tuo.	It's yours.
È mio.	It's mine.
È nostro.	It's ours.
È per te.	It's for you.

QUIZ 8

1. È molto.	1. It's enough.
2. È facile.	2. That isn't true.
3. È vicino.	3. It's bad.
4. È abbastanza.	4. It's near.
5. Questo non è vero.	5. It's mine.
6. È male.	6. It's true.
7. È piccolo.	7. It's here.
8. È vero.	8. It's small.
9. È mio.	9. It's easy.
10. È qui.	10. It's a lot.

ANSWERS

1-10; 2-9; 3-4; 4-1; 5-2; 6-3; 7-8; 8-6; 9-5; 10-7.

LESSON 10

24. TO HAVE and HAVE NOT

(Simple Sentences II)

TO HAVE

io ho	I have
tu hai	you have
egli ha	he has
noi abbiamo	we have

| *voi avete* | you have |
| *essi hanno* | they have |

NOT TO HAVE

io non ho	I don't have
tu non hai	you don't have
egli non ha	he doesn't have
noi non abbiamo	we don't have
voi non avete	you don't have
essi non hanno	they don't have
Io ho tempo.	I have time.
Io non ho tempo.	I haven't any time.
Egli non ha amici.	He hasn't any friends.
Ha (lei) una sigaretta?	Do you have a cigarette?
Io ho fame.	I'm hungry (I have hunger).
Ilo sete. (Io ho sete.)	I'm thirsty. (I have thirst.)
Ho freddo. (Io ho freddo.)	I'm cold. (I have cold.)
Ho caldo. (Io ho caldo.)	I'm warm. (I have warmth.)
Ho ragione.	I'm right. (I have reason.)

25. I KNOW ONLY A LITTLE ITALIAN

Parla italiano? Parla lei italiano?	Do you speak Italian?
Sì, un poco.	Yes, a little.
Molto poco.	Very little.
Non molto bene.	Not very well.
Io parlo italiano.	I speak Italian.
Lo parlo male.	I speak it poorly.
Io non lo parlo molto bene.	I don't speak it very well.
Io conosco solo poche parole.	I know only a few words.

So dire poche parole in italiano.	I know how to say a few words in Italian.
Il suo amico parla italiano?	Does your friend speak Italian?
No, il mio amico non parla italiano.	No, my friend doesn't speak Italian.
Comprende l'italiano?	Do you understand Italian?
Sì, comprendo l'italiano.	Yes, I understand Italian.
Lo comprendo ma non lo parlo.	I understand it, but I don't speak it.
Lo leggo ma non lo parlo.	I read it but I don't speak it.
No, io non comprendo l'italiano.	No, I don't understand Italian.
Io non comprendo molto bene l'italiano.	I don't understand Italian very well.
Non lo pronuncio molto bene.	I don't pronounce it very well.
Mi manca la practica.	I lack practice.
Ho bisogno di practica.	I need practice.
Lei mi comprende?	Do you understand me?
Io la comprendo.	I understand you.
Io non la comprendo molto bene.	I don't understand you very well.
Che cosa ha detto?	What did you say?
Lei parla troppo in fretta.	You speak too fast. (You speak in too much of a hurry.)
Lei parla troppo veloce.	You are speaking too fast.
Non parli cosi in fretta.	Don't speak so fast.
Parli più lentamente.	Speak more slowly.
Per favore, parli più lentamente.	Please, speak a little more slowly.

Mi scusi, ma non la capisco. Non l'ho capita.	Excuse me, but I don't understand. I didn't understand you.
Per favore, me lo ripeta.	Please, say it again (to me).
Mi comprende ora?	Do you understand me now?
Oh, ora capisco.	Oh, now I understand.
Che cosa significa in italiano?	What does that mean in Italian?
Come si dice "Thanks" in italiano?	How do you say "Thanks" in Italian?
Come si scrive questa parola?	How do you spell (write) that word?
Per favore, me la scriva.	Please, write it down for me.

LESSON 11

26. DO YOU SPEAK ITALIAN?

(Conversational Forms)

Buon giorno, signore.	Good morning, (sir).
Buon giorno.	Good morning.
Lei parla italiano?	Do you speak Italian?
Sì, io parlo italiano.	Yes, I speak Italian.
Io non parlo inglese.	I don't speak English.
È (lei) italiano?	Are you an Italian?
Sì, io sono italiano.	Yes, I am Italian.
Da quanto tempo è lei negli Stati Uniti?	How long have you been in the United States?
Da tre mesi.	Three months.
Lei imparerà presto l'inglese.	You'll soon learn English.
Lei imparerà l'inglese in poco tempo. Non è molto difficile.	You'll learn English in a little time. It's not very hard.

É più difficile di quello che pensa.	It's harder than you think.
Forse lei ha ragione.	You are probably right. (Perhaps you have reason.)
È più facile per noi imparare l'italiano che per voi l'inglese.	Italian is easier for us to learn than English is for you. (For us it is easier to learn Italian than for you, English.)
Lei parla italiano molto bene.	You speak Italian very well.
Io ho vissuto in Italia per diversi anni.	I lived in Italy for several years.
Lei ha un'ottima pronuncia.	You have an excellent pronunciation.
Molte grazie, ma mi manca la pratica. Ho bisogno di pratica.	Thank you, but I lack practice. I need practice.
Adesso devo andare. Il mio treno sta per partire.	I have to leave now. My train's about to leave.
Buona fortuna e buon viaggio.	Good luck and a pleasant trip.
Altrettanto.	The same to you.
Addio.	Good-by.

QUIZ 9

1. *Lo comprendo ma non lo parlo.*	1. Do you speak Italian?
2. *Mi comprende ora?*	2. I need practice.
3. *Non lo parlo molto bene.*	3. A little.
4. *Lei parla troppo in fretta.*	4. What did you say?
5. *Come si scrive questa parola?*	5. Say it again.
6. *Lei parla italiano?*	6. Not very well.

7. *Ho bisogno di pratica.*	7. I didn't understand very well.
8. *Un poco.*	8. I understand it but I don't speak it.
9. *Me lo ripeta.*	9. Speak more slowly.
10. *Non molto bene.*	10. I don't speak it very well.
11. *Parli più lenta-mente.*	11. How do you say "Thanks" in Italian?
12. *Lo parlo male.*	12. You speak too fast.
13. *Che cosa ha detto?*	13. Do you understand me now?
14. *Come si dice "Thanks" in italiano?*	14. How do you spell that word?
15. *Non ho capito bene.*	15. I speak it poorly.

ANSWERS

1-8; 2-13; 3-10; 4-12; 5-14; 6-1; 7-2; 8-3; 9-5; 10-6;
11-9; 12-15; 13-4; 14-11; 15-7.

27. EXCUSE ME

Mi scusi.	Pardon me. Excuse me.
Le chiedo scusa.	I beg your pardon.
Mi scusi.	Excuse me.
Per favore, ripeta. Mi vuole fare il favore di ripetere?	Please repeat. Will you do me the favor of repeating it?
Con piacere.	With pleasure. Gladly.
Con molto piacere.	With the greatest pleasure.
Sono a sua disposizione.	I'm at your disposal.
Che cosa posso fare per lei?	What can I do for you? (In what can I serve you?)

Lei è molto gentile.	You are very kind. That's very kind of you.
Lei è molto cortese.	You are very kind. (You are very courteous.)
Grazie.	Thanks.
Molte grazie.	Many thanks.
Grazie infinite.	Thanks a lot. (Very many thanks.)
Mille grazie.	Thanks very much. (A thousand thanks.)
Di nulla.	Don't mention it. (Of nothing.)
Non c'è di che.	Don't mention it. (Nothing at all.)
Niente affatto.	It's nothing. (Nothing at all.)

LESSON 12

28. THIS and THAT

(This, More, And)

Dammi questo.	Give me this one *(masc.)*.
Dammi questa.	Give me this one *(fem.)*.
Dammi questi.	Give me these *(masc.)*.
Dammi queste.	Give me these *(fem.)*.
Dammi quello.	Give me that one *(masc.)*.
Dammi quella.	Give me that one *(fem.)*.
Dammi quelli.	Give me those *(masc.)*.
Dammi quelle.	Give me those *(fem.)*.
Dammi quello là.	Give me that one over there. *(Refers to something farther away.)*

Dammi quella là.	Give me that one *(fem.)* over there.
Dammi quelli là.	Give me those over there.
Dammi quelle là.	Give me those *(fem.)* over there.

When *questo* and *quello* are used as adjectives preceding nouns, the forms of *questo* are as above, but *quello* has a different set of endings:

questo ragazzo	this boy
questa signora	this lady
quel signore là	that gentleman over there
quella signora	that lady
quello sbaglio	that mistake
quei vicini	those neighbors
quegli studenti	those students

QUIZ 10

1. *Dammi questi.*	1. Give me those over there.
2. *questo*	2. that one over there
3. *Dammi quella.*	3. this lady
4. *questo ragazzo*	4. this one
5. *quello*	5. that gentleman over there
6. *quei vicini*	6. this boy
7. *Dammi quelli là.*	7. Give me these.
8. *quello là*	8. that one
9. *questa signora*	9. those neighbors
10. *quel signore là*	10. Give me that one *(fem.)*.

ANSWERS

1-7; 2-4; 3-10; 4-6; 5-8; 6-9; 7-1; 8-2; 9-3; 10-5.

29. MORE or LESS

1. More

più piano	more slowly
più difficile	more difficult
più facile	easier
più lontano	farther
più vicino	nearer
più di quello	more than that
più di un anno	more than a year

2. Less

meno piano	less slowly
meno difficile	less difficult
meno facile	less easy
meno lontano	less far, not so far
meno vicino	less near, not so near
meno di quello	less than that
meno di un anno	less than a year

REVIEW QUIZ 2

1. _____ (this) *ragazzo*
   a. *questa*
   b. *questo*
   c. *queste*

2. *Dammi* _____ (those, *fem.*).
   a. *quelle*
   b. *queste*
   c. *questo*

3. *Ho* _____ (here) *i libri.*
   a. *egli*
   b. *qui*
   c. *come*

4. *Venga* _____ (here).
   a. *ella*
   b. *lì*
   c. *qui*

5. *Domani vado* _____ (there).
   a. *lì*
   b. *noi*
   c. *come*

6. _____ (Where) *sta?*
   a. *Là*
   b. *Dove*
   c. *Qui*

7. *È* _____ (far) *da qui?*
   a. *lontano*
   b. *quella*
   c. *lì*

8. *Roberto* _____ (and) *Giovanni sono fratelli.*
   a. *con*
   b. *e*
   c. *più*

9. *cinque* _____ (or) *sei lire*
   a. *o*
   b. *e*
   c. *più*

10. *Desidero venire* _____ (but) *non posso.*
    a. *o*
    b. *ma*
    c. *fino*

ANSWERS

1-b; 2-a; 3-b; 4-c; 5-a; 6-b; 7-a; 8-b; 9-a; 10-b.

30. AND, OR and BUT

1. *e* "and"

Roberto e Giovanni sono fratelli.	Robert and John are brothers.

ed is used instead of *e* before nouns beginning with a vowel:

Roberto ed Andrea sono fratelli.	Robert and Andrew are brothers.

2. *o* "or"

cinque o sei lire	five or six lire
sette o otto ore	seven or eight hours

3. *ma* "but"

Egli non è francese ma inglese.	He is not French but English.
Engli non viene oggi ma domani.	He is not coming today but tomorrow.

QUIZ 11

1. *inglese*	1. five or six days
2. *e*	2. He is not French but English.
3. *ma*	3. seven or eight hours
4. *figlia*	4. English
5. *fratello*	5. but
6. *cinque o sei giorni*	6. tomorrow
7. *quando*	7. daughter
8. *Egli non è francese ma inglese.*	8. and
9. *domani*	9. when
10. *sette o otto ore*	10. brother

ANSWERS

1-4; 2-8; 3-5; 4-7; 5-10; 6-1; 7-9; 8-2; 9-6; 10-3.

LESSON 13

31. WHERE?

(Where, Here, There)

Dov'è?	Where is it?
Qui.	Here.
Lì.	There.
A destra.	To the right.
A sinistra.	To the left.
All'angolo.	On the corner.
È in via Condotti.	It's in Via Condotti.
Si trova in via Condotti.	(via = street)
È in piazza Venezia.	It's in Piazza Venezia.
Si trova in piazza Venezia.	(piazza = square)

È in viale Mazzini. Si trova in viale Mazzini.	It's in Viale Mazzini, (viale = avenue)
Per dove? Per quale strada?	Which way?
Per questa strada. Per questa via.	This way.
Per quella strada. Per quella via.	That way.
Come si arriva lì?	How do you get there?
Vada sempre avanti.	Go straight ahead.
Giri a destra. Svolti a destra.	Turn to your right.
Giri a sinistra. Svolti a sinistra.	Turn to your left.
Dov'è questo posto?	Where's the place you're talking about?
Dove si trova?	Where is it?
È qui.	It's here.
È proprio qui.	It's right here.
È lì.	It's there.
È più lontano	It's farther.
È un po' più lontano.	It's a little farther.
È lontano?	Is it far?
Quanto è lontano da qui?	How far is it from here to there?
È vicino.	It's near.
Non è troppo lontano.	It's not too far.
È lontano de qui?	Is it far from here?
Dov'è il libro?	Where's the book?
È qui.	It's here.
È proprio qui.	It's right here.
È lì.	It's there (where you are).

È lì.	It's over there (distant from both of us).
Dov'è lei?	Where are you?
Sono qui.	Here I am.
Egli è qui.	Here he is.
Egli è qui. Egli si trova qui.	He's here.
Egli è lì.	He's there.
Eccolo che va via. Eccolo che se ne va.	There he is, going away.
È lì, da qualche parte.	It's somewhere over there.
Lo metta qui.	Put it here.
Lo metta lì.	Put it there.
Mi aspetti qui.	Wait for me here.
Mi aspetti lì.	Wait for me there.
Venga qui.	Come here.
Eccolo che viene.	Here he comes.
Vada lì.	Go there.
Fino a lì.	Way over there.
Qui intorno. Qui vicino.	Around here. Near here.

LESSON 14

(Here, There, Pronouns)

1. Here and There:

lì in Italia	over there in Italy
qui in America	here in America
Dove abita egli?	Where does he live?
Egli abita lì.	He lives there.
Io spero di vederlo lì.	I expect to see him there.
Ella è lì.	She's there.
Giovanni abita qui?	Does John live here?

È qui.	This is the place. It's here.
Non è qui.	It's not here.
È lì.	It's there.
Prenda questa strada.	Go this way.
Prenda quella strada.	Go that way.
Venga per questa strada.	Come this way.
Vada di lì.	Go that way.
Ho i libri qui.	I have the books here.
Cosa hai lì?	What do you have there?
Sei lì?	Are you there?

2. Near and Far:

qui vicino	near here
molto vicino	very near
a pochi passi da qui	a few steps from here
vicino al paese	near the town
vicino al parco	near the park
vicino alla chiesa	next to the church
È lontano?	Is it far?
È lontano da qui?	Is it far from here?
È molto lontano.	It's very far.
Non è molto lontano.	It's not too far.
È a due caseggiati da qui.	It's two blocks from here.
È a un miglio da qui.	It's a (one) mile from here.

QUIZ 12

1. *lì in Italia.*	1. I expect to see him there.
2. *Aspettami qui.*	2. in there.
3. *qui*	3. to the left
4. *a destra*	4. It's far.

5. *lì*	5. here
6. *È proprio qui.*	6. Wait for me here.
7. *Io spero di vedero lì.*	7. straight ahead.
8. *a sinistra*	8. to the right
9. *È lontano.*	9. there
10. *lì dentro*	10. Go there.
11. *È lì, da qualche parte.*	11. Go that way.
12. *È vicino.*	12. It's right here.
13. *Vada lì.*	13. over there in Italy
14. *Vada per quella strada*	14. It's somewhere around there.
15. *sempre avanti.*	15. It's near.

ANSWERS

1-13; 2-6; 3-5; 4-8; 5-9; 6-12; 7-1; 8-3; 9-4; 10-2;
11-14; 12-15; 13-10; 14-11; 15-7.

32. I, YOU, HE

The use of the subject pronouns is optional: "I speak" is just *parlo;* "we speak," *parliamo;* etc. But the pronouns are used for emphasis or clearness:

Io studio, tu ti diverti.	I study, *you* enjoy yourself.
La signora pensa che io goda buona salute.	The lady thinks that *I* enjoy good health.

1. I, You, He.	Singular
io	I
tu	you *(familiar)*
egli	he
ella	she
lei	you *(polite)*

io parlo	I speak
tu parli	you speak *(familiar)*
egli parla	he speaks
ella parla	she speaks
lei parla	you speak *(polite)*

PLURAL

noi	we
voi	you
essi	they *(masc.)*
esse	they *(fem.)*
loro	they, you *(polite)*

noi parliamo	we speak
voi parlate	you speak
essi parlano	they speak
esse parlano	they speak *(fem.)*
loro parlano	they speak, you speak *(polite)*

2. It's I.

Sono io.	It's I.
Sei tu.	It's you.
È lui.	It's he.
È lei.	It's she.
Siamo noi.	It's we.
Siete voi.	It's you.
Sono loro.	It's they
	It's you *(polite pl.)*

3. My, Yours, His.

il mio amico	my friend
mio, -a, -ei, -e	my
tuo, -a, -oi, -e	your *(fam.)*
suo, -a, -oi, -e	his, her, your *(polite)*
nostro, -a, -i, -e	our
vostro, -a, -i, -e	your *(fam. pl.)*
loro	their, your *(polite pl.)*

In Italian the possessive adjective is always preceded by the definite article, except when it comes before members of the family in the singular. *Loro* is always preceded by the article.

tuo fratello	your brother
mia figlia	my sister
il loro figlio	their son

LESSON 15

(Useful Phrases and Idioms)

Study the following examples:

SINGULAR

il mio amico	my friend
il tuo amico	your friend
il suo amico	his, her, your friend
il nostro amico	our friend
la nostra amica	our friend *(fem.)*
il vostro amico	your friend
la vostra amica	your friend
il loro amico	their friend, your friend

PLURAL

i miei amici	my friends
i tuoi amici	your friends
i suoi amici	his, her, your friends
i nostri amici	our friends
le nostre amiche	our friends *(fem.)*
i vostri amici	your friends
le vostre amiche	your friends *(fem.)*
i loro amici	their friends, your friends

SINGULAR

il mio cappello	my hat
il tuo vestito	your dress
il suo vestito	her dress
il nostro amico	our friend
il nostra borsa	our bag
il vostro cavallo	your horse
la vostra penna	your pen

PLURAL

i miei cappelli	my hats
i tuoi vestiti	your dresses
i suoi vestiti	her dresses
i nostri amici	our friends
le nostre borse	our bags
i vostri cavalli	your horses
le vostre penne	your pens

4. It's mine.

È mio.	It's mine.
È tuo.	It's yours.
È suo.	It's his (hers, yours).
È nostro.	It's ours.
È vostro.	It's yours.
È il loro.	It's theirs.
È il mio.	It's mine.
È il tuo.	It's yours.
È il suo.	It's his (hers, yours).
È il nostro.	It's ours.
È il vostro.	It's yours.
È il loro.	It's theirs.

Other examples:

i miei amici ed i tuoi	my friends and yours
Il suo libro è migliore del nostro.	His book is better than ours.

Di chi è questa lettera? Whose is this letter? It's
   Sua.   his.

Notice the form of the pronoun when it comes after a preposition:

SINGULAR

per me	for me
per te	for you
con lui	with him
a lei	to her
a te	for you

PLURAL

senza noi	without us
con voi	with you
per loro	for them *(masc.)*
per loro	for them *(fem.)*
di voi	of you

5. He sees me.

Egli me vede.	He sees me.
Egli ti vede.	He sees you.
Io lo vido.	I see him.
Io la vido.	I see her.
Io la vido.	I see you *(polite)*.
Essi ci vedono.	They see us.
Noi li vediamo.	We see them *(masc.)*.
Noi le vediamo.	We see them *(fem.)*.
Noi li vediamo.	We see you *(polite)*.

Generally the article is used with the possessive; however, in some cases it is omitted.

6. About me.

Io parlo di te.	I'm speaking about you.
Tu parli di me.	You *(fam.)* are speaking about me.
Egli parla di lui.	He is speaking about him.
Ella parla di lei.	She is speaking about her.
Noi parliamo di voi.	We are speaking about you *(pl.)*.
Voi parlate di noi.	You *(pl.)* are speaking about us.
Essi parlano di loro.	They are speaking about them.

7. He tells it to me.

Egli lo dice a me.	He tells it to me.
Egli lo dice a te.	He tells it to you *(sing.)*.
Egli lo dice a lui.	He tells it to him.
Egli lo dice a lei.	He tells it to her.
Egli lo dice a noi.	He tells it to us.
Egli lo dice a voi.	He tells it to you.
Egli lo dice a loro.	He tells it to them.

8. He gives it to me.

Egli me lo dà.	He gives it to me.
Egli te lo dà.	He gives it to you.
Egli glielo dà.	He gives it to him.
Egli glielo dà.	He gives it to her.
Egli ce lo dà.	He gives it to us.
Egli ve lo dà.	He gives it to you.
Egli lo dà loro.	He gives it to them.

Notice the change in the form of some of the pronouns according to their position in the sentence.

9. It and Them.

SINGULAR	PLURAL
Masculine *lo* it	*li* them
Feminine *la* it	*le* them

Ha il denaro?	Do you have the money?
Sì io l'ho. (l' stands for lo)	Yes, I have it.
Ha la borsetta?	Do you have the handbag?
Sì, io l'ho. (l' stands for la)	Yes, I have it.
Ha visto Pietro e Giovanni?	Have you seen Peter and John?
Sì, io li ho visti.	Yes, I have seen them.
Ha visto Maria e Luisa?	Have you seen Mary and Louise?
Sì, io le ho viste.	Yes, I saw them.

Notice that the pronoun agrees with the word it refers to. *Lo* and *la* elide; *li* and *le* do not. *Lo* is used when the reference is to an idea or a whole expression:

Lo capisco.   I understand it.

Lo, la, etc. usually come immediately before the verb, as in the case of other object pronouns. However, they are added to the infinitive:

Voglio capirlo.   I want to understand it.

10. I'm speaking to you.

Io le parlo.	I'm speaking to you *(polite).*
Egli ti parla.	He is speaking to you.
Egli le parla.	He is speaking to you *(polite).*

11. Myself, Yourself.

Io mi lavo.	I wash myself.

Tu ti lavi.	You wash yourself.
Egli si lava.	He washes himself.
Ella si lava.	She washes herself.
Lei si lava.	You wash yourself *(polite).*
Noi ci laviamo.	We wash ourselves.
Voi vi lavate.	You wash yourselves.
Loro si lavano.	They wash themselves.

Other examples:

Come si chiama?	What's your name? (How do you call yourself?)
Noi ci vediamo nello specchio.	We see ourselves in the mirror.
Essi si scrivono.	They write to one another.

12. Notice the forms for "myself," "yourself," etc.: *mi, ti, si,* etc. Verbs which take these "reflexive pronouns" are called "reflexive" verbs. Many verbs are reflexive in Italian which are not in English:

Mi diverto.	I'm having a good time.
Mi siedo.	I sit down. I'm sitting down.
Mi alzo.	I get up. I'm getting up (standing up).
Mi dimentico.	I forget.
Mi ricordo.	I remember.
Mi fermo.	I stop.
M'addormento.	I fall asleep.

13. In Italian you don't say "I'm washing my hands," but "I'm washing the hands"; "Take your hat off," but "Take off the hat":

Io mi lavo le mani.	I'm washing my hands.
Si tolga il cappello.	Take your hat off.
Egli si è rotto il braccio.	He broke (has broken) his arm.

Ella si è tagliato il dito.	She's cut her finger.
Mi sono fatto male alla mano.	I've hurt my hand.
Mi fa male la testa. Ho mal di testa.	I have a headache.
Mi fa male lo stomaco. Ho mal di stomaco.	I have a stomach-ache.
Sto perdendo la pazienza.	I'm losing my patience.

14. The reflexive forms are often used where we would use the passive in English:

Qui si parla italiano.	Italian is spoken here.
Le porte si aprono alle otto.	The doors are opened at eight.

The reflexive forms are also often used to translate our "one," "they," "people," etc.

Si dice che...	It's said that... People say that... They say that...
Qui si mangia bene.	The food's good here. (One eats well here.)

QUIZ 13

1. *Mi siedo.*	1. I get up.
2. *M'addormento.*	2. I stop.
3. *Mi diverto.*	3. I forget.
4. *Mi ricordo.*	4. I'm mistaken.
5. *Mi alzo.*	5. I wash myself.
6. *Mi lavo.*	6. I'm having a good time.
7. *Mi sbaglio.*	7. They write to each other.
8. *Si scrivono.*	8. I remember.
9. *Mi dimentico.*	9. I fall asleep.

10. *Mi fermo.*   10. I sit down.

ANSWERS

1-10; 2-9; 3-6; 4-8; 5-1; 6-5; 7-4; 8-7; 9-3; 10-2

REVIEW QUIZ 3

1. *È* _____ (he).
   a. *egli*
   b. *lui*
   c. *io*

2. *Siamo* _____ (we).
   a. *loro*
   b. *tu*
   c. *noi*

3. *Io do il libroa* _____ (him).
   a. *lui*
   b. *voi*
   c. *loro*

4. *il* _____ (her) *vestito*
   a. *suo*
   b. *mio*
   c. *nostro*

5. *la* _____ (our) *carta*
   a. *nostro*
   b. *nostra*
   c. *tuo*

6. *Dove sono i* _____ (my) *libri?*
   a. *tuoi*
   b. *miei*
   c. *nostri*

7. *Il suo libro è migliore del* _____ (ours).
   a. *tuoi*
   b. *nostro*
   c. *suoi*

8. *Parliamo di* _____ (him).
   a. *te*
   b. *essi*
   c. *lui*

9. *Egli* _____ (to us) *lo dice*.
   a. *lui*
   b. *ce*
   c. *voi*

10. *Come si* _____ (call) *lei?*
    a. *lava*
    b. *chiama*
    c. *vede*

11. *Noi ci* _____ (wash).
    a. *lava*
    b. *lavano*
    c. *laviamo*

12. *Mi* _____ (to be mistaken).
    a. *sbaglio*
    b. *lavo*
    c. *giro*

13. *Mi* _____ (sit down).
    a. *vado*
    b. *ricordo*
    c. *siedo*

14. *Mi sono* _____ (hurt) *alla mano*.
    a. *sbagliato*
    b. *lavo*
    c. *fatto male*

15. *Egli* _____ (leaving, going away).
    a. *se ne va*
    b. *veniamo*
    c. *chiamo*

ANSWERS

1-b; 2-c; 3-a; 4-a; 5-b; 6-b; 7-b; 8-c; 9-b; 10-b; 11-c; 12-a; 13-c; 14-c; 15-a.

LESSON 16

33. A FEW SHORT PHRASES

(Important Phrases, Questions, Numbers)

Stia attento! Attenzione!	Watch out!
Faccia attenzione! Attento!	Be careful! Watch out!
Presto!	Fast! Hurry up!
Vada presto! Corra!	Go fast! Run!
Più presto!	Faster!
Non tanto di corsa.	Not so fast. (Don't run so much.)
Non molto in fretta. Non di corsa.	Not very fast. Not in a hurry.
Più piano. Senza fretta.	Slower. With no hurry.
Meno in fretta.	Slower.
Vengo. Io vengo. Sto venendo.	I'm coming.
Vengo subito. Corro.	I'm coming right away.
Corra. Faccia presto.	Hurry up.
Non c'è fretta. Non corra.	Don't hurry.
Io ho fretta.	I'm in a hurry.
Non ho fretta (Io).	I'm not in a hurry.
Un momento!	Just a minute! In a minute!
All'istante. Subito. Immediatamente.	Right away. Immediately.
Venga subito! Corra!	Come right away.
Presto.	Soon.
Immediatamente.	Immediately.
Più presto.	Sooner.
Più tardi.	Later.

QUIZ 14

1. *Stia attento!* *Attenzione!*	1. Slower.
2. *Io ho fretta.*	2. Right away.
3. *Un momento!*	3. Come right away!
4. *Presto.*	4. I'm coming!
5. *Immediatamente.*	5. Watch out!
6. *Più tardi.*	6. Later.
7. *Più piano.*	7. I'm in a hurry.
8. *Vengo! Sto venendo!*	8. Just a minute! In a minute!
9. *Venga subito!* *Corra!*	9. Immediately.
10. *All'istante. Subito.*	10. Soon.

ANSWERS

1-5; 2-7; 3-8; 4-10; 5-9; 6-6; 7-1; 8-4; 9-3; 10-2.

34. MAY I ASK . . . ?

Posso farle una domanda?	May I ask you a question?
Posso domandarle . . . ? **Posso chiederle . . . ?**	May I ask (you) . . . ?
Può dirmi?	Can you tell me?
Potrebbe dirmi?	Could you tell me?
Mi vuol dire?	Will you tell me?
Potrebbe dirmi, per favore?	Could you please tell me?
Vuol farmi il piacere di dirmi?	Could you please tell me?
Che cosa vuol dire?	What do you mean?
Io voglio dire che . . .	I mean that . . .

Che cosa significa questo?	What does that mean?
Questo significia . . .	This means . . .

35. NUMBERS

1. *One, Two, Three . . .*

uno	one
due	two
tre	three
quattro	four
cinque	five
sei	six
sette	seven
otto	eight
nove	nine
dieci	ten
undici	eleven
dodici	twelve
tredici	thirteen
quattordici	fourteen
quindici	fifteen
sedici	sixteen
diciassette	seventeen
diciotto	eighteen
diciannove	nineteen
venti	twenty
ventuno	twenty-one
ventidue	twenty-two

LESSON 17

(Numbers II)

ventitrè	twenty-three
trenta	thirty

trentuno	thirty-one
trentadue	thirty-two
trentatrè	thirty-three
quaranta	forty
quarantuno	forty-one
quarantadue	forty-two
quarantatrè	forty-three
cinquanta	fifty
cinquantuno	fifty-one
cinquantadue	fifty-two
cinquantatrè	fifty-three
sessanta	sixty
sessantuno	sixty-one
sessantadue	sixty-two
sessantatrè	sixty-three
settanta	seventy
settantuno	seventy-one
settantadue	seventy-two
settantatrè	seventy-three
ottanta	eighty
ottantuno	eighty-one
ottantadue	eighty-two
ottantatrè	eighty-three
novanta	ninety
novantuno	ninety-one
novantadue	ninety-two
novantatrè	ninety-three
cento	hundred
centuno	a hundred and one
centodue	a hundred and two
centotrè	a hundred and three
mille	thousand
milledue	a thousand and two
milletrè	a thousand and three

2. *Some More Numbers*

cento venti	120

cento ventidue	122
cento trenta	130
cento quaranta	140
cento cinquanta	150
cento sessanta	160
cento settanta	170
cento settantuno	171
cento settantotto	178
cento ottanta	180
cento ottantadue	182
cento novanta	190
cento novantotto	198
cento novantanove	199
duecento	200
trecento ventiquattro	324
ottocento settantacinque	875

LESSON 18

(Counting, Currency)

3. *First, Second, Third . . .*

primo	-a, -i, -e	first
secondo	-a, -i, -e	second
terzo	-a, -i, -e	third
quarto	-a, -i, -e	fourth
quinto	-a, -i, -e	fifth
sesto	-a, -i, -e	sixth
settimo	-a, -i, -e	seventh
ottavo	-a, -i, -e	eighth
nono	-a, -i, -e	ninth
decimo	-a, -i, -e	tenth

4. *Two and Two*

due e due fanno quattro	two and two are four

due più due fanno quattro	two and two are four
quattro più due fanno sei	four and two are six
dieci meno due fanno otto (dieci meno due otto)	ten minus two is eight

QUIZ 15

1.	*mille*	1.	1002
2.	*undici*	2.	32
3.	*cento*	3.	102
4.	*diciassette*	4.	324
5.	*trenta*	5.	11
6.	*venti*	6.	1000
7.	*sessanta*	7.	60
8.	*trecento ventiquattro*	8.	71
9.	*trentadue*	9.	17
10.	*centodue*	10.	875
11.	*ottocento settantacinque*	11.	83
12.	*settantuno*	12.	93
13.	*mille e due*	13.	20
14.	*novantatrè*	14.	30
15.	*ottantatrè*	15.	100

ANSWERS

1-6; 2-5; 3-15; 4-9; 5-14; 6-13; 7-7; 8-4; 9-2; 10-3; 11-10; 12-8; 13-1; 14-12; 15-11

36. HOW MUCH?

| **Quanto costa questo?** | How much does this cost? |
| **Costa quaranta lire.** | It costs forty lire. |

Quanto costa una libbra di caffè?	How much is a pound of coffee?
Costa cinquecento lire.	It costs 500 lire.

37. IT COSTS...

Costa...	It costs...
Questo libro costa duecento lire.	This book costs 200 lire.
Egli ha comprato un automobile per duemila dollari.	He bought a car for two thousand dollars.
Il viaggio in treno da Roma a Milano costa seimila lire.	The trip by train from Rome to Milan costs six thousand lire.
Ho risparmiato ventidue dollari per comprarmi un abito.	I've saved twenty-two dollars to buy a suit.
Egli ha guadagnato nel mese di guigno cinquemila ottocento trentaquattro lire.	He made 5,834 lire in the month of June.
Si vende solamente alla libbra e costa trecento lire.	It's sold only by the pound and costs 300 lire.

LESSON 19

38. MY ADDRESS IS...

(Addresses, Dates)

Io abito in via Nazionale numero duecento cinquanta.	I live at 250 Nazionale Street.

Ella abita al corso Italia numero trecento.	She lives at 300 Corso d'Italia.
Il negozio si trova in viale Mazzini numero trecento ventisei.	The store is at 326 Mazzini Avenue.
Essi si sono trasferiti in piazza Venezia novecento ventuno.	They moved to 921 Venezia Square.

39. MY TELEPHONE NUMBER IS...

Il mio numero di telefono è sei tre due otto otto.	My telephone number is 63288.
Il loro numero di telefono è quattro zero otto sei zero.	Their telephone number is 40860.
Non dimentichi il mio numero di telefono: otto sei cinque zero sei.	Don't forget my telephone number: 86506.
Signorina, mi dia il numero quattro zero tre sei nove.	Operator, may I have 40369?
Il numero cinque sei otto sette cinque non risponde.	Number 56875 doesn't answer.

40. THE NUMBER IS...

Il numero è...	The number is...
Il mio numero è...	My number is...
Il numero della mia camera è trenta.	My room number is 30.
Io abito nella camera numero trenta.	I live in room 30.

Il numero della mia casa è mille trecento ventidue.	My address (house number) is 1322.
Io abito al numero trecento trentadue del viale Quinto, al quinto piano.	I live at 332 Fifth Avenue, fifth floor.

41. WHAT'S TODAY?

Che giorno della settimana è oggi?	What's today? (What day of the week is today?)
È lunedì.	Monday.

The following expressions all mean "What's the date?":

Quanti ne abbiamo?	(How many days do we have?)
A che data siamo oggi?	(At what date are we today?)
Che giorno è oggi?	(What day is today?)
Siamo al venti. E il venti. Ne abbiamo venti.	It's the 20th. (We're at the 20th.)
il primo di maggio	the 1st of May
l'undici aprile	the 11th of April
il quattro luglio	the 4th of July
il quindici settembre	the 15th of September
il ventuno giugno	the 21st of June
il venticinque dicembre	the 25th of December
il diciassette novembre	the 17th of November
il tredici febbraio	the 13th of February
i ventotto agosto	the 28th of August

LESSON 20

42. SOME DATES

(Dates II, Time I)

L'America fu scoperta nel mille quattrocento novantadue.	America was discovered in 1492.
"I Promessi Sposi" furono pubblicati nel mille ottocento venticinque.	"I Promessi Sposi" ("The Betrothed") was published in 1825.
Dante nacque nel mille duecento sessantacinque, e morì nel mille trecento ventuno.	Dante was born in 1265, and died in 1321.
Noi siamo stati lì nel mille novecento cinquantadue, o nel mille novecento cinquantatrè.	We were there in 1952; or in 1953.
Cosa avvenne nel mille novecento quarantuno?	What happened in 1941?
Il presidente Roosevelt morì nel mille novecento quarantacinque.	President Roosevelt died in 1945.

QUIZ 16

1. È lunedì.	1. the 25th of June
2. Che giorno del mese è oggi?	2. the 28th of February
3. il primo di luglio	3. the 13th of August
4. Che giorno è oggi?	4. 1605
5. l'undici aprile	5. It's Monday.

6. *il ventotto febbraio*	6. What day of the month is it?
7. *il venticinque giugno*	7. date
8. *mille seicento cinque*	8. the first of July
9. *il tredici agosto*	9. the 11th of April
10. *data*	10. What's the date?

ANSWERS

1-5; 2-6; 3-8; 4-10; 5-9; 6-2; 7-1; 8-4; 9-3; 10-7.

43. WHAT TIME IS IT?

Che ora è?	What time is it?
È l'una.	1:00 o'clock.
È l'una e cinque.	1:05.
È l'una e dieci.	1:10.
È l'una e quindici.	1:15.
È l'una e un quarto.	1:15.
È l'una e mezza.	1:30.
È l'una e cinquanta.	1:50.
Sono le due meno dieci.	1:50 (ten minutes to two).
Sono le due.	2:00.
Sono le tre.	3:00.
Sono le quattro.	4:00.
Sono le cinque.	5:00.
Sono le sei.	6:00.
Sono le sette.	7:00.
Sono le otto.	8:00.
Sono le nove.	9:00.
Sono le dieci.	10:00.
Sono le undici.	11:00.
Sono le dodici.	12:00 noon. It's noon.
È mezzogiorno.	12:00. It's noon.
È mezzanotte.	12:00 midnight. It's midnight.

minuto	minute
ora	hour
A che ora?	(At) what time?
Che ora è, per favore?	Can you please tell me the time?
Ha l'ora, per favore?	Do you have the time, please?
Il mio orologio fa le cinque.	It's 5 o'clock by my watch. (My watch marks 5 o'clock.)

LESSON 21

(Time II)

Sono le tre e dieci.	It's 3:10.
Sono le sei e mezza.	It's 6:30.
Sono le due meno un quarto.	It's a quarter to 2.
Non sono ancora le quattro.	It's not four yet.
A che ora parte il treno?	What time does the train leave?
Alle nove in punto. **Alle nove precise.**	At 9 o'clock sharp. Exactly at 9 o'clock.
Alle nove circa. Verso le nove.	About 9 o'clock. Around 9 o'clock.
Sono le dieci della mattina.	It's 10 A.M.
Alle tre meno venti del pomeriggio.	At 2:40 P.M. (Twenty minutes to three.)
Alle quindici meno venti.	At 2:40 P.M.
Alle sei di sera.	At 6 P.M.
Alle diciotto	At 6 P.M.
Alle sei del pomeriggio.	At 6 P.M.

Notice that when you want to specify "A.M." or "P.M." in Italian, you add *della mattina, del pomeriggio, di sera,* or you may count 24 hours in the day, so that 15 o'clock would stand for 3 P.M.

44. IT'S TIME

È ora.	It's time.
È ora di farlo.	It's time to do it.
È ora di partire.	It's time to leave.
È ora di andare a casa.	It's time for us to go home.
Ho molto tempo.	I have a lot of time.
Non ho tempo.	I haven't any time.
Egli sta perdendo il tempo. Perde il tempo.	He is wasting his time.
Egli viene di tanto in tanto.	He comes from time to time.

QUIZ 17

1. *È ora di farlo.*	1. He comes from time to time.
2. *Che ora è?*	2. It's 9:00.
3. *È l'una.*	3. At what time?
4. *Sono le tre.*	4. It's time to do it.
5. *Sono le nove.*	5. It's 2:00
6. *È mezzanotte.*	6. It's 1:00.
7. *A che ora?*	7. I haven't any time.
8. *Non ho tempo.*	8. It's 2:40 P.M. (Twenty minutes to 3.)
9. *È l'una e un quarto.*	9. It's noon.
10. *Sono le quattro.*	10. It's 3:00.

11. *Sono le due.*   11. It's 1:05.
12. *Egli viene di tanto*   12. It's 4:00.
    in tanto.
13. *È mezzogiorno.*   13. What time is it?
14. *È l'una e cinque.*   14. It's 1:15.
15. *Sono le tre meno*   15. It's midnight.
    venti del
    pomeriggio.

ANSWERS

1-4; 2-13; 3-6; 4-10; 5-2; 6-15; 7-3; 8-7; 9-14;
10-12; 11-5; 12-1; 13-9; 14-11; 15-8

45. PAST, PRESENT AND FUTURE

Passato	Presente	Futuro
ieri	**oggi**	**domani**
yesterday	today	tomorrow
ieri mattina	**questa mattina**	**domani mattina**
yesterday	**(stamatina)**	tomorrow
morning	this morning	morning
ieri sera	**questa sera**	**domani sera**
last evening	**(stasera)**	tomorrow
	this evening	evening
ieri notte	**questa notte**	**domani notte**
last night	**(stanotte)**	tomorrow
	tonight	night

46. MORNING, NOON AND NIGHT

questa mattina (stamattina)	this morning
ieri mattina	yesterday morning
domani mattina	tomorrow morning
questo pomeriggio	this afternoon
ieri pomeriggio	yesterday afternoon
domani pomeriggio	tomorrow afternoon
questa sera (stasera)	this evening
ieri sera	yesterday evening
domani sera	tomorrow evening
questa notte (stanotte)	tonight
ieri notte	last night
domani notte	tomorrow night

LESSON 22

(Time III)

questa settimana	this week
la settimana passata	last week
la settimana scorsa	last week
la settimana entrante	next week
la settimana prossima	next week
in due settimane	in two weeks
due settimane fa	two weeks ago
questo mese	this month
il mese passato	last month
il mese entrante	next month
il mese che viene	the month that's coming
in due mesi	in two months
due mesi fa	two months ago
quest'anno	this year
l'anno passato	last year
l'anno prossimo	next year
l'anno che viene	next year

in due anni	in two years
fra due anni	the year after next
due anni fa	two years ago
Quanto tempo fa?	How long ago?
un momento fa	a moment ago
molto tempo fa	a long time ago
ora	now, for the time being
in questo preciso momento	this very moment
da un momento all'altro	at any moment
per il momento	for the time being
in questo momento	at this moment
in breve tempo	in a short time
in poco tempo	in a little while
di tanto in tanto	from time to time
Quante volte?	How many times?
una volta	once
ogni volta	each time
due volte	twice
raramente	very seldom
non spesso	not often
molte volte (molto spesso)	very often
a volte (qualche volta)	sometimes
ogni tanto	once in a while
di tanto in tanto	{ now and then from time to time
di mattina presto	early in the morning
al crepuscolo	in the evening (twilight)
al l'imbrunire	at nightfall
il giorno seguente	on the following day
il giorno dopo	on the following day
fra due settimane	two weeks from today
fra una settimana	a week from today
domani a otto	a week from tomorrow
in una settimana	in a week
mercoledì prossimo	next Wednesday

il lunedì della settimana passata	Monday a week ago
il cinque di questo mese	the fifth of this month
il cinque del mese passato	the fifth of last month
al principio di marzo	at the beginning of March
alla fine del mese	at the end of the month
al principio dell'anno	in the early part of the year
verso la fine dell'anno	towards the end of the year
Avvenne otto anni fa.	It happened eight years ago.

QUIZ 18

1.	*ieri mattina*	1.	last year
2.	*questa sera*	2.	last night
3.	*domani sera*	3.	today at noon
4.	*ieri notte*	4.	now
5.	*il mese entrante*	5.	in two weeks
6.	*ora*	6.	in a little while
7.	*la settimana passata*	7.	yesterday morning
8.	*l'anno passato*	8.	from time to time
9.	*oggi a mezzogiorno*	9.	It happened eight years ago.
10.	*in poco tempo*	10.	this evening
11.	*questa settimana*	11.	sometimes
12.	*Avvenne otto anni fa.*	12.	within a week
13.	*verso la fine dell'anno*	13.	tomorrow evening
14.	*due mesi fa*	14.	next month
15.	*verso la fine del mese*	15.	last week
16.	*in una settimana*	16.	each time
17.	*di tanto in tanto*	17.	about the end of the month

18. *a volte*
18. toward the end of the year

19. *in due settimane*
19. this week

20. *ogni volta*
20. two months ago

ANSWERS

1-7; 2-10; 3-13; 4-2; 5-14; 6-4; 7-15; 8-1; 9-3; 10-6;
11-19; 12-9; 13-18; 14-20; 15-17; 16-12; 17-8;
18-11; 19-5; 20-16

REVIEW QUIZ 4

1. *Compro un'automobile per* _____ (four thousand) *dollari.*
   a. *tremila*
   b. *quattrocento*
   c. *quattromila*

2. *Il numero del suo telefono è* _____ (40860).
   a. *sei, cinque, zero, sei, nove*
   b. *tre, sei, nove, due, zero*
   c. *quattro, zero, otto, sei, zero*

3. *Che* _____ (date) *abbiamo?*
   a. *giorno*
   b. *mese*
   c. *data*

4. *Che* _____ (day) *è oggi?*
   a. *mese*
   b. *giorno*
   c. *come*

5. *il* _____ (17) *dicembre*
   a. *dicisassette*
   b. *ventisette*
   c. *cinque*

6. *È* _____ (1:10).
   a. *l'una e cinque*
   b. *l'una e dieci*
   c. *l'una e un quarto*

7. *Sono le* _____ (7).
   a. *sette*
   b. *nove*
   c. *sei*

8. *È* _____ (12 noon).
   a. *mezzanotte*
   b. *mezzogiorno*
   c. *undici*

9. *Sono le* _____ (2:40).
   a. *le quattro meno un quarto*
   b. *le tre meno venti*
   c. *le due meno un quarto*

10. _____ (yesterday) *mattina*
    a. *oggi*
    b. *ieri*
    c. *e*

11. *la* _____ (week) *passata*
    a. *settimana*
    b. *notte*
    c. *domani*

12. *fra due* _____ (months)
    a. *settimana*
    b. *giorno*
    c. *mesi*

13. *Sono due* _____ (years).
    a. *mesi*
    b. *anni*
    c. *giorni*

14. *il* _____ (Wednesday) *della settimara entrante*
    a. *lunedì*
    b. *venerdì*
    c. *mercoledì*

15. *alla* _____ (end) *dell'anno*
    a. *fine*
    b. *principio*
    c. *primo*

ANSWERS

1-c; 2-c; 3-c; 4-b; 5-a; 6-b; 7-a; 8-b; 9-b; 10-b; 11-a;
12-c; 13-b; 14-c; 15-a.

LESSON 23

47. NO, NOT

(No, Not)

The word for "not," *non,* comes before the verb:

io non vedo	I don't see
tu non vedi	you don't see
Non vedo nulla.	I see nothing.
	I don't see anything.
Non vado mai.	I never go.
Non vengono.	They don't come.
	Nobody comes.
Non vedo niente.	I see nothing.
	I don't see anything.
Non vado mai via.	I never go away.
Nessuno viene (non viene nessuno).	No one is coming (nobody comes).
Sì, signore.	Yes, sir.
No, signore.	No, sir.
Dice di sì.	He says yes.
Dice di no.	He says no.
Credo di sì.	I think so.
Non è bene.	It's not good.
Non è male.	It's not bad.
Non è quello.	It's not that.
Non è qui.	He's not here.
È qui.	It's here.
Non è troppo.	It's not too much.

Non è abbastanza.	It's not enough.
È abbastanza.	It's enough.
Non tanto in fretta. Non così in fretta.	Not so fast.
Non tanto spesso. Non così spesso.	Not so often.
Non è nulla. È nulla.	It's nothing.
Questo è nulla. Ciò è nulla.	That's nothing.
Non è molto importante.	It's not very important.
Non ho tempo.	I have no time.
Non so nè come nè dove.	I don't know how or where.
Non so dove.	I don't know where.
Non so nulla. Non so niente.	I don't know anything.
Non ne so nulla. Non so nulla di ciò.	I know nothing about it.
Non voglio nulla. Non desidero nulla.	I don't want anything.
Non importa. Non fa nulla.	It doesn't matter. It's not important.
Non me ne importa.	I don't care. It makes no difference to me.
Non me ne importa nulla. Non me ne importa affatto.	I don't care at all. It doesn't make the slightest difference to me.
Non lo dica.	Don't say it.
Non ho nulla da dire.	I've nothing to say.
Non lo dirò mai.	I'll never say it.
Non è successo nulla.	Nothing happened.
Non ho hulla da fare.	I have nothing to do.
Non lo vedo mai.	I never see him.
Non l'ho mai visto prima.	I've never seen him before.

Non l'ho mai visto.	I've never seen him.
Non viene mai.	He never comes.
Non è mai venuto.	He has never come.
Non vado mai.	I never go.
Non andrò mai.	I'll never go.

LESSON 24

(Nor, Word Groups)

Nè = Nor

Non ho detto una parola, nè una sillaba.
I haven't said a word, nor a syllable.
Non posso andare nè voglio andare.
I can't go, nor do I want to go.
Nè...nè...
Neither...nor...
Nè più nè meno.
Just so (neither more nor less).
Nè l'uno nè l'altro.
Neither the one nor the other. (Neither one).
Nè questo nè quello.
Neither this nor that.
Nè molto nè poco.
Neither much nor little.
Nè bene nè male.
Just so so. Neither good nor bad.
Non ho nè tempo nè denaro.
I have neither the time nor the money.
Non sa nè leggere nè scrivere.
He (she) can neither read nor write.
Non ho nè sigarette nè fiammiferi.
I have neither cigarettes nor matches.

48. USEFUL WORD GROUPS

1. Isn't it?

È vero?
Is it?
Non è vero?
Isn't it?
L'italiano è facile, non è vero?
Italian is easy, isn't it?
La gente qui è molto gentile, non è vero?
The people here are very nice, aren't they?
Lei non ha una matita, vero?
You don't have a pencil, do you?
Lei conosce questo posto, non è vero?
You know this place, don't you?
Lei conosce il signor Rossi, non è vero?
You know Mr. Rossi, don't you?
Lei ha un cucchiaio e un tovagliolo, non è vero?
You have a spoon and a napkin, haven't you?
Lei non è qui da molto tempo, non è vero?
You haven't been here very long, have you?
Lei verrà, non è vero?
You will come, won't you?
Fa freddo, non è vero?
It's cold, isn't it?
È molto carino! Non è carino?
Isn't it cute! It's cute, isn't it?
Va bene, non è vero?
It's all right, isn't it?

2. Some, Any, A Few

Ha (lei) del denaro?
Do you have any money?
Sì, ne ho.
Yes, I have some.
No, non ne ho.
No, I don't have any.

Ha (egli) del denaro?
Does he have any money?
Ne ha.
He has some.
Non ne ha affatto.
He doesn't have any at all.
Ha ancora del denaro? Le è rismasto del denaro?
Do you still have money? Do you have any money left?
Me ne è rimasto un po'.
I have some left. (Some remains to me.)
Quanti libri ha?
How many books do you have?
Ne ho pochi.
I have few.
Desidera un po' di frutta?
Do you want some fruit?
Me ne dia un po'.
Give me some.

QUIZ 19

1. *Non vedo.*	1. Neither this nor that.
2. *Non è nulla.*	2. I have no time.
3. *Non lo dirò mai.*	3. Don't tell it to me.
4. *Non vado mai via.*	4. Nothing happened.
5. *Egli non vede Giovanni.*	5. I don't see.
6. *Non credo.*	6. I don't know anything.
7. *Non tanto in fretta.*	7. I've never seen him.
8. *Non so nulla.*	8. He doesn't see John.
9. *Non vedo nulla.*	9. I'll never say it.
10. *Io non l' ho mai visto.*	10. He never comes.
11. *Non me ne importa.*	11. I see nothing.

12. *Non è successo nulla.*	12. I'll never go.
13. *Egli non viene mai.*	13. It's nothing.
14. *Non è male.*	14. He's not here.
15. *Non andrò mai.*	15. I don't think so.
16. *Non è qui.*	16. It's not bad.
17. *Nessuno viene.*	17. I don't care.
18. *Nè questo nè quello.*	18. Not so fast.
19. *Non me lo dica.*	19. I never go away.
20. *Non ho tempo.*	20. No one comes.

ANSWERS

1-5; 2-13; 3-9; 4-19; 5-8; 6-15; 7-18; 8-6; 9-11;
10-7; 11-17; 12-4; 13-10; 14-16; 15-12; 16-14;
17-20; 18-1; 19-3; 20-2.

LESSON 25

(Like, As, Conversation)

Ce ne dia un po'.
Give us some.
Ne dia un po' a lui.
Give him some.
alcuni dei miei amici.
some of my friends.

   3. Like, As, How

     Come = like, as, how
     come me
     like me
     come quello
     like that
     come questo
     like this
     come noi
     like us

come gli altri
like the others
Questo non è come quello.
This one isn't like that one.
Ecco com' è.
That's how it is.
Come desidera.
As you wish.
È come a casa propria.
It's like (being at) home.
Egli non è come suo padre.
He's not like his father.
Non so come spiegare.
I don't know how to explain.
Com' è?
What does it look like? (How is it?)
È bianco come la neve.
It's as white as snow.
Come piove!
What rain! (How it's raining!)
Come? Cosa dice?
What? What did you say? What do you mean?
Perchè no? Come no?
Why not? Yes, of course.

QUIZ 20

1. *Come desidera.*	1. He's not like his father.
2. *come gli altri*	2. What? What did you say?
3. *come questo*	3. Give him some.
4. *Ha (lei) del denaro?*	4. Why not?
5. *alcuni dei miei amici*	5. Do you want some fruit?
6. *Non è come suo padre.*	6. As you wish.
7. *Come?*	7. Do you have any money?
8. *Ne dia un po' a lui.*	8. like the others

9. *Perchè no?*
9. like this

10. *Desidera un po' di frutta?*
10. some of my friends

ANSWERS

1-6; 2-8; 3-9; 4-7; 5-10; 6-1; 7-2; 8-3; 9-4; 10-5.

49. HAVE YOU TWO MET?

Conosce il mio amico?
Do you know my friend?
Credo che ci siamo già conosciuti.
I believe we've met before.
Non credo di aver avuto il piacere.
I don't believe I've had the pleasure.
Non ho avuto il piacere di conoscerla.
I haven't had the pleasure (of meeting you).
Credo che loro si conoscano già, non è vero?
I think you already know each other, don't you? (I believe you already know each other, don't you?)
Credo che ci conosciamo.
I think we know each other.
Non ho avuto il piacere.
I haven't had the pleasure.
Ho già avuto il piacere di conoscerlo.
I've already had the pleasure of meeting him.
Mi permetta di presentarla al mio amico Antonio de Marchi.
Allow me to introduce you to my friend Antonio de Marchi.

50. SMALL TALK

Buon giorno.
Good morning. Good afternoon. Good day.
Come sta?
How do you do? How are you getting along?

Non c'è male. E lei?
So, so. And you?
E come sta lei?
And how are you getting along?
Che c'è di nuovo?
What's new?
Niente di nuovo.
Nothing much.
Che novità?
What's new?
Nulla di importante.
Nothing much.

LESSON 26

(Conversation, Taking Leave)

C'è niente di nuovo?
(Is there) anything new?
Non c'è niente di nuovo.
There's nothing new.
Com'è che non la si vede mai?
Where have you been? (What has happened that no
    one ever sees you?)
Sono stato molto occupato in questi giorni.
I've been very busy these days.
Mi telefoni qualche volta.
Give me a ring sometime.
Le telefonerò uno di questi giorni.
I'll phone you one of these days.
Perchè non viene a trovarci a casa?
Why don't you come to see us (to our house)?
Verrò a trovarvi la settimana entrante.
I'll call on you next week. (I'll come to visit you next
    week).

Non dimentichi la sua promessa.
Now don't forget your promise.
Alla prossima settimana, allora.
Until next week, then.
Arrivederci alla settimana entrante.
See you next week. (Until next week.)

51. TAKING LEAVE

Sono lieto di averla conosciuta.
Glad to have met you.
Molto lieto.
Glad (happy) to have met you. (Charmed.)
Spero di vederla presto.
Hope to see you again soon.
Lo spero anch'io.
I hope so, too.
Ecco il mio indirizzo e il mio numero di telefono.
Here's my address and telephone number.
Ha il mio indirizzo?
Do you have my address?
No, me lo dia.
No, let me have it.
Eccolo qui.
Here it is.
Molte grazie.
Thanks.
Quando posso telefonarle?
When can I phone you?
Di mattina.
In the morning.
La chiamerò dopodomani.
I'll call you the day after tomorrow.
Aspetterò la sua chiamata.
I'll be expecting your call.

Arrivederci.
So long.
Arrivederla a presto.
See you soon.
A più tardi.
So long. See you later.
Arrivederci ad un'altra volta.
So long. See you again. (Until another time.)
A domani.
See you tomorrow. (Till tomorrow.)
A sabato.
See you Saturday. (Till Saturday.)
Addio.
Good-by.

QUIZ 21

1. *Spero di veder la presto.*
2. *Arriveder la.*
3. *Sono lieto di aver la conosciuta.*
4. *Ha il mio indirizzo?*
5. *Eccolo qui.*
6. *Di mattina.*

7. *A domani.*
8. *Aspetterò la sua chiamata.*
9. *Molte grazie.*
10. *A sabato.*

1. Do you have my address?
2. See you tomorrow.
3. I'll be expecting your call.
4. Till Saturday.
5. In the morning.
6. Glad to have met you.
7. Thanks a lot.
8. Hope to see you soon.
9. Here it is.
10. Good-by.

ANSWERS

1-8; 2-10; 3-6; 4-1; 5-9; 6-5; 7-2; 8-3; 9-7; 10-4.

LESSON 27

52. CALLING ON SOMEONE

(Visiting, Letters)

Abita qui il signor Giovanni Rossi?
Does Mr. John Rossi live here?
Sì, abita qui.
Yes, he does. (He lives here.)
A che piano?
On what floor?
Terzo piano a sinistra.
Third floor left.
È in casa il signor Rossi?
Is Mr. Rossi at home?
No signore. È uscito.
No, Sir. He's gone out.
A che ora sarà di ritorno? A che ora ritornerà?
What time will he be back?
Non, so dirle.
I can't tell you.
Desidera lasciar detto qualche cosa?
Do you want to leave him a message?
**Gli lascerò un biglietto, se mi può dare una matita
   e un pezzo di carta.**
I'll leave him a note, if you can give me a pencil and a
   piece of paper.
Ritornerò questa sera.
I'll come back tonight.
Ritornerò domani.
I'll come back tomorrow.
Ritornerò un altro giorno.
I'll come back another day.
Gli dica di telefonarmi, per favore.
Please tell him to phone.
Sarò in casa tutto il giorno.
I'll be at home all day.

53. LETTERS AND TELEGRAMS

Vorrei scrivere una lettera.
I'd like to write a letter.

Mi può dare un po' di carta?
Could you let me have (give me) some paper?

Qui c'è carta e inchiostro.
Here is some paper and ink.

Vado all'ufficio postale.
I'm going to the post office.

Dove si vendono i francobolli?
Where are stamps sold?

Ha francobolli?
Do you have stamps?

Ho bisogno di un francobollo aereo.
I need an airmail stamp.

Qui ci sono dei francobolli.
Here are some stamps.

Un francobollo espresso, per favore.
A special·delivery stamp, please.

Dov'è la cassetta delle lettere? (Dov'è la buca delle lettere?)
Where is the mailbox?

Devo spedire un telegramma.
I have to send a telegram.

Quanto costa un telegramma per Genova?
How much does a telegram to Genoa cost?

QUIZ 22

1. *terzo piano a sinistra.*
2. *Ritornerò più tardi.*

1. I'll be at home all day.
2. Do you have stamps?

3. *Abita qui il signor Giovanni Rossi?*	3. I'd like to write a letter.
4. *Qui c'è carta e inchiostro.*	4. Where is the mailbox?
5. *Vorrei scrivere una lettera.*	5. What floor?
6. *Ha francobolli?*	6. a special delivery stamp
7. *Che piano?*	7. Here is some paper and ink.
8. *un francobollo espresso*	8. Does Mr. John Rossi live here?
9. *Sarò in casa tutto il giorno.*	9. third floor left
10. *Dov'è la cassetta postale?*	10. I'll come back later.

ANSWERS

1-9; 2-10; 3-8; 4-7; 5-3; 6-2; 7-5; 8-6; 9-1; 10-4.

54. GETTING AROUND

Dov'è questa strada?
Where is this street?
Come si arriva a questo posto?
How do you get to this place?
È molto lontano?
Is it very far?
Qual'è la via più breve per andare a Torino?
What's the shortest way to get to Torino?
Quale strada devo prendere?
Which road must I take?
Puo indicarmi dov'è via Veneto?
Can you direct me to Veneto Street?

È qui vicino via Barberini?
Is Barberini Street near here?

LESSON 28

(Traveling)

Dove c'è un telefono pubblico?
Where is there a public phone?

Dove posso telefonare?
Where can I phone?

Quanto è lontana da qui la stazione?
How far away is the station from here?

Quanto è lontana la stanzione?
How far is the station?

Siamo ancora lontani dalla stazione?
Are we still far from the station?

Tassì!
Taxi!

È libero?
Are you taken? (Are you free?)

Mi porti a questo indirizzo.
Take me to this address.

Quanto le devo?
How much do I owe you?

Si ferma qui l'autobus?
Does the bus stop here?

Si ferma qui il tram?
Does the streetcar stop here?

A che fermata devo scendere?
At what stop do I get off?

QUIZ 23

1. *Qual'è la via più breve per andare a . . . ?*
2. *Dove posso telefonare?*
3. *Dov'è questa strada?*
4. *Mi porti a questo indirizzo.*
5. *Quanto è lontana la stazione?*
6. *Posso usare il suo telefono?*
7. *Può indicarmi dov'è via . . . ?*
8. *A che fermata devo scendere?*
9. *Come si arriva a questo posto?*
10. *Si ferma qui l'autobus?*

1. How far is the station?
2. How do you get to this place?
3. Can you direct me to . . . Street?
4. Does the bus stop here?
5. At what stop do I get off?
6. Where can I phone?
7. Where is this street?
8. What's the shortest way to get to . . . ?
9. Take me to this address.
10. May I use your phone?

ANSWERS
1-8; 2-6; 3-7; 4-9; 5-1; 6-10; 7-3; 8-5; 9-2; 10-4.

55. PLEASE

The commonest ways of saying "please" are *per favore,* or *mi faccia il favore,* which literally means: do me the favor of. Notice how the pronouns are used:

Mi faccia il favore di portare questo.
Please carry this.

Mi faccia il favore di venire.
Please come. (Do me the favor of coming.)

Ci faccia il favore di entrare.
Please come in. (Do us the favor of coming in.)

Facciano il favore di entrare.
Please come in. (Speaking to several people.)

Per favore, mi faccia vedere i suoi documenti.
Please let me see your papers.

Per favore, vuol chiamare un tassì?
Will you please call a taxi?

56. SOME OTHER USEFUL POLITE EXPRESSIONS

1. **Abbia la bontà.**
   Please. (Have the goodness.)

   Abbia la bontà di dirmi dov'è la stazione.
   Can you tell me, please, where the station is?

2. **Mi scusi. Mi perdoni.**
   Excuse me. Pardon me.

   Scusi il ritardo.
   Excuse my lateness.

3. **Per cortesia.**
   Please.

   Per cortesia, il suo biglietto.
   Your ticket, please.

   Per cortesia, sieda qui.
   Please sit here.

4. **La prego.**
   Please. (I pray you.)

   La prego di farlo al più presto possibile.
   Please do it as soon as possible.

La prego, puo dirmi dov'è la biblioteca?
Can you please tell me where the library is?

QUIZ 24

1. *Per favore, sieda qui.*
2. *Per favore, venga qui.*
3. *Per favore, vuol chiamare un tassì?*
4. *Scusi il mio ritardo.*
5. *Mi scusi. Mi perdoni.*
6. *Per favore, voglia entrare.*
7. *Per favore, può dirmi dov'è la stazione?*
8. *Per favore, porti questo.*
9. *Per favore, il suo biglietto.*
10. *Per favore, mi dica dov'è la biblioteca.*

1. Excuse my lateness.
2. Excuse me. Pardon me.
3. Please come here.
4. Please carry this.
5. Please tell me where the library is.
6. Your ticket, please.
7. Will you please call a taxi?
8. Please come in.
9. Can you please tell me where the station is?
10. Please sit here.

ANSWERS

1-10; 2-3; 3-7; 4-1; 5-2; 6-8; 7-9; 8-4; 9-6; 10-5.

LESSON 29

(Who? What? Why?)

Io devo andare.	I have to leave.

C'è (ci è) means "there is" or "there are":

C'è molta gente qui.	There are a lot of people here.

Desidero, or *desidererei,* means "I should like to":

Desidera sedere qui?	Would you like to sit here?
Desidererei andare, ma non posso.	I'd like to go, but I can't.

REVIEW QUIZ 5

1. *È in* _____ *(home, house) il signor Rossi?*
   a. *appartamento*
   b. *ora*
   c. *casa*

2. *Desidera lasciare un* _____ *(note)?*
   a. *matita*
   b. *biglietto*
   c. *carta*

3. *Dov'è questa* _____ *(street)?*
   a. *luogo*
   b. *cammino*
   c. *strada*

4. _____ *(I need) di un francobollo aereo.*
   a. *Vendere*
   b. *Ho bisogno*
   c. *Subito*

5. _____ (Who) *ha detto questo?*
   a. *A chi*
   b. *Chi*
   c. *Di lui*

6. _____ (Because) *non desidero perdere il treno.*
   a. *Perchè*
   b. *Che*
   c. *Chi*

7. *Di* _____ (what) *parlano?*
   a. *perchè*
   b. *cosa*
   c. *desidera*

8. _____ (What) *desidera?*
   a. *Perchè*
   b. *Che*
   c. *Quale*

9. *Abbia la* _____ *di dirmi dov'è la stazione.*
   a. *mi scusi*
   b. *bontà*
   c. *faccia*

10. *Mi facciano il* _____ *di entrare.*
    a. *bontà*
    b. *piacere*
    c. *servire*

11. _____ (Please) *lo faccia al più presto possibile.*
    a. *Servire*
    b. *Mi scusi*
    c. *Per piacere*

12. *Ha la faccia bianca* _____ (as) *la neve.*
    a. *cui*
    b. *come*
    c. *questo*

13. _____ (I should like), *ma non posso.*
    a. *Io desidererei*
    b. *Ho*
    c. *Desidera*
14. _____ (Why) *non lo ha detto?*
    a. *Chi*
    b. *Perchè*
    c. *Di chi*

ANSWERS

1-c; 2-b; 3-c; 4-b; 6-a; 7-b; 8-b; 9-b; 10-b; 11-c;
12-b; 13-a; 14-b.

57. WHO? WHAT? WHEN?

1. *Chi?* = Who?

Chi è?	Who is he (she)?
Non so chi è.	I don't know who he is.
Chi sono?	Who are they?
Chi lo ha detto?	Who said it?
Chi l' ha detto?	Who said so?
Chi l' ha fatto?	Who did it?
Di chi è questa matita?	Whose pencil is this?
Per chi è questo?	Who is this for?
Chi desidera vedere?	Whom do you wish to see?
A chi desidera parlare?	To whom do you wish to speak?
Chi lo sa?	Who knows it?
Di chi è questo?	Whose is this?

2. *Che? Che cosa?* = What?

Che cosa è questo?	What's this?
Che cosa è quello?	What's that?
Che cosa succede?	What's the matter? What's up?

Che c'è?	What's the matter? What's up?
Che è successo?	What happened?
Ch c'è di nuovo?	What's new?
Cosa pensa? Che cosa pensa?	What do you think?
Cosa sono?	What are they?
Che cosa ha? Cosa le succede?	What do you have? What's the matter with you?
Che ora è?	What time is it?
Che cosa dice?	What are you saying?
Che cosa ha detto?	What did you say?
Di che cosa sta parlando?	What are you talking about?
Di che si tratta?	What's it all about?
Che cosa vuole?	What do you want?
Cosa posso fare per lei?	What can I do for you? What do you wish?

3. *Perchè?* = Why?

Perchè così?	Why so?
Perchè no?	Why not?
Perchè dice questo?	Why do you say that?
Perchè tanta fretta?	Why are you in such a hurry? Why the hurry?
Perchè l' ha fatto?	Why did you do it?
Perchè non viene?	Why don't you come?

4. *Come?* = How?

Come si dice questo in italiano?	How do you say this in Italian?
Come si chiama?	What is your name? (How do you call yourself?)

| **Come si scrive questo?** | How is this (written) spelled? |

5. *Quanto?* = How much?

Quanto denaro desidera?	How much money do you want?
Quanti libri ci sono?	How many books are there?
Quanto è distante Napoli da Firenze?	How far is it from Naples to Florence?

LESSON 30

(What? Where? When?)

6. *Quale?* = What? Which?

Qual'è il suo nome?	What is his name?
Quale desidera?	Which (one) do you want?
Quale desidera, questo o quello?	Which (one) do you want, this one or that one?
Quale di queste matite è la sua?	Which one of these pencils is yours?
Quale di queste due strade conduce a Siena?	Which of these two roads leads to Siena?
Qual'è il suo indirizzo?	What's his address? (or) What's your address?

7. *Dove?* = Where?

Dov'è il suo amico?	Where is your friend?
Dove vive (egli)?	Where does he live?
Dove và (ella)?	Where is she going?

8. *Quando?* = When?

Quando verrà suo fratello?	When will your brother come?
Quando è successo?	When did that happen?
Quando parte?	When are you going (leaving)?
Non so quando.	I don't know when.
Fino a quando? Per quanto tempo?	Until when? How long?
Non so fino a quando.	I don't know how long. (I don't know until when.)
Quando? Fra quanto tempo?	When?
Quando lei vuole.	When you wish.
Da quando?	Since when?
Com'è avvenuto?	How did it happen?
Quando è accaduto?	When did it happen?
Da quando è qui?	How long have you been here?

QUIZ 25

1. *Come si chiama?*	1. When did that happen?
2. *Quanti libri ci sono?*	2. Since when?
3. *Come si dice questo in italiano?*	3. Who knows?
4. *Che cosa dice?*	4. Where does he live?
5. *Quando è successo?*	5. What's your name?
6. *Da quando?*	6. What are you saying?
7. *Chi lo sa?*	7. Why not?
8. *Perchè no?*	8. How do you write that?
9. *Dove abita (egli)?*	9. How many books are there?

10. *Come si scrive guesto?*

10. How do you say this in Italian?

ANSWERS

1-5; 2-9; 3-10; 4-6; 5-1; 6-2; 7-3; 8-7; 9-4; 10-8.

REVIEW QUIZ 6

1. *Non vedo* _____ (nothing).
   a. *nessuno*
   b. *nulla*
   c. *mai*

2. *Non viene* _____ (nobody).
   a. *nessuno*
   b. *no*
   c. *mai*

3. *Non sa leggere* _____ (nor) *scrivere.*
   a. *no*
   b. *mai*
   c. *nè*

4. *L'italiano è facile,* _____ (isn't it)?
   a. *non è vero*
   b. *è vero*
   c. *no*

5. *Me ne dia* _____ (a little).
   a. *nulla*
   b. *un po'*
   c. *qualcosa*

6. *Desidera* _____ (some) *di frutta?*
   a. *alcuni*
   b. *pochi*
   c. *un po'*

7. *Non è* _____ (like) *suo padre.*
   a. *come*
   b. *è*
   c. *gi altri*

8. *È stato molto _____ (busy) in questi giorni.*
   a. *sempre*
   b. *occupato*
   c. *nuovo*

9. *Si _____ (know) loro?*
   a. *conosciuti*
   b. *conoscono*
   c. *conoscerla*

10. *Con chi ho il piacere di _____ (speak)?*
    a. *parlare*
    b. *avere*
    c. *conoscere*

11. *Ecco il mio _____ (address) ed il mio numero di telefono.*
    a. *giorno*
    b. *biglietto*
    c. *indirizzo*

12. *Ci vedremo uno di questi _____ (days).*
    a. *giorni*
    b. *molto*
    c. *settimana*

13. *Lei ha la _____ (mine).*
    a. *molto*
    b. *mia*
    c. *giorno*

14. *_____ (What) dice?*
    a. *Come*
    b. *Quando*
    c. *Che*

15. *_____ (Why) è andata via?*
    a. *Che cosa*
    b. *Perchè*
    c. *Quanto*

16. _____ (How) *si dice questo in italiano?*
   a. Come
   b. Quando
   c. Nessuno

17. _____ (How much) *denaro desidera?*
   a. A chi
   b. Quanto
   c. Di chi

18. _____ (Who) *ha il suo vino?*
   a. Chi
   b. Di chi
   c. Quale

19. _____ (Where) *il suo amico?*
   a. Dov'è
   b. Come
   c. Chi

20. _____ (When) *verrà suo fratello?*
   a. Chi
   b. Quale
   c. Quando

ANSWERS

1-b; 2-a; 3-c; 4-a; 5-b; 6-c; 7-a; 8-b; 9-b; 10-a; 11-c;
12-a; 13-b; 14-c; 15-b; 16-a; 17-b; 18-a; 19-a; 20-c.

58. LIKING AND DISLIKING

1. *I like it.*

Mi piace.   I like it.
Buono.   Good.

Molto buono.	Very good.
È molto buono.	It's very good.
È eccellente.	It's excellent.
È stupendo.	It's wonderful.
È magnifico.	It's excellent. It's wonderful.
È ammirabile.	It's excellent. It's admirable.
È perfetto.	It's perfect.
È giusto.	It's all right.
Non c' è male.	It's not bad.
Va bene?	Is it all right?
Molto bene. Molto buono.	Very well. Very good.
È bella.	She's beautiful.
È bellissima.	She's very beautiful.
È molto carina.	She's very pretty.
È attraente.	She's charming.
Com'è carino!	How pretty!
Com'è grazioso!	How pretty!
Com'è buono!	How nice!
Com'è bello!	How beautiful!

2. *I don't like it.*

Non è buono.	It's not good. It's no good.
Non è molto buono.	It's not very good.
Quello non è buono.	That's no good.
Questo non è giusto.	It's not right. This isn't right.
Questo non è corretto.	This isn't proper. This is wrong.
È male.	That's bad.
È molto male.	It's very bad.
È pessimo.	That's very bad. That's awfully bad.

È fatto malissimo.	It is done very badly.
È veramente cattivo.	It's really (truly) bad.
Non mi interessa.	I don't care for it. It doesn't interest me.
Non mi piace.	I don't like it.
Non mi piace affatto.	I don't like it at all.

LESSON 31

(Like, Dislike)

Questo non vale niente.	That's worthless.
Non serve a nulla.	It's worthless. It's good for nothing.
Che peccato!	What a pity!
Che disgrazia!	How unfortunate! (What a misfortune!)
Che orrore!	How awful!

QUIZ 26

1. *Va bene.*	1. It's excellent.
2. *Molto bene.*	2. She's very pretty.
3. *È eccellente.*	3. That's worthless.
4. *Non c'è male.*	4. What a pity!
5. *È male.*	5. How unfortunate!
6. *Che peccato!*	6. It's wonderful!
7. *È molto carina.*	7. It's all right.
8. *Non serve a nulla.*	8. That's bad.
9. *Che disgrazia!*	9. Very well.
10. *È stupendo.*	10. It's not bad.

ANSWERS

1-7; 2-9; 3-1; 4-10; 5-8; 6-4; 7-2; 8-3; 9-5; 10-6.

3. I like . . .

Mi piace . . .	I like . . . (It pleases me . . .)
Mi piace molto.	I like it (him, her) very much.
Mi piace moltissimo.	I like it (him, her) very much.
Mi piace quello.	I like that.
Ella mi piace.	I like her.
Mi piacciono molto.	I like them a lot.
Le piace?	Do you like it?
Non le piace?	Don't you like it?
Le piace la frutta?	Do you like fruit?
Sì, la frutta mi piace.	Yes, I like fruit.
Le piace la cioccolata?	Do you like chocolate?
Le piace l'America?	Do you like America?
Le piace la cucina italiana?	Do you like Italian food?
Le piace l'Italia?	Do you like Italy?
Le è piaciuta l'Italia?	Did you like Italy?
L'Italia mi è piaciuta.	I liked Italy.
Crede che la casa piacerà loro?	Do you think they'll like the house?
Come piace loro la mia camera?	How do you like my room? (speaking to several people)
Mi piace.	I like it.
Mi piace molto.	I like it very much.
Non mi piace.	I don't like it.
Non mi piace molto.	I don't like it very much.
Se le piace.	If you like it.
Quando le piace. Quando desidera.	Whenever you like.
La musica mi piace molto.	I'm fond of music.

Notice that the Italian for "I like fruit" is *Mi piace la frutta* (To me is pleasing fruit). That is, the word which is the object in English is the subject in Italian. "I like the United States" is *Mi piacciono gli Stati Uniti* (To me are pleasing the United States). Here the verb is plural because the subject is plural.

QUIZ 27

1. *Le piace la cucina italiana?*	1. I don't like it very much.
2. *Le piace?*	2. Do you like my room?
3. *Mi piace molto.*	3. Do you like Italy?
4. *Le piace la frutta?*	4. If you like it.
5. *Quando le piace.*	5. Don't you like it?
6. *Le piace l'Italia?*	6. I like it very much.
7. *Non le piace?*	7. Do you like it?
8. *Se le piace.*	8. Whenever you like.
9. *Non mi piace molto.*	9. Do you like Italian food?
10. *Le piace la mia camera?*	10. Do you like fruit?

ANSWERS

1-9; 2-7; 3-6; 4-10; 5-8; 6-3; 7-5; 8-4; 9-1; 10-2.

59. IN, TO, FROM

Abito in Italia.	I live in Italy.
Sono stato a Roma.	I've been in Rome.
Vado a Roma.	I'm going to Rome.
Vengo da Roma.	I come (am) from Rome.
Parto per Roma.	I'm leaving for Rome.
Egli va verso Roma.	He's going towards Rome.
Sono andato fino a Roma.	I went as far as Rome.
Vado in Europa.	I am going to Europe.

1. **A = To**

a destra	to the right
a sinistra	to the left
due a due	two by two
poco a poco	little by little
a piedi	on foot
a mano	by hand
a mezzogiorno	at noon
a mezzanotte	at midnight
Si sedettero a tavola.	They sat down at the table.
all' italiana	in the Italian manner
A domani.	Until tomorrow.
A presto.	See you soon. (Until soon.)
A più tardi.	See you later. (Until later.)
Arrivederci. Alla prossima volta.	Good-by. Until we see each other again.

LESSON 32

(With, From)

2. **Con = With**

caffè con latte	coffee with milk
Io andai con Giovanni.	I went with John.
Egli lo ha scritto con una matita.	He wrote it with a pencil.

3. **Di = Of, From**

È di mio fratello.	It's my brother's.
Io sono di Roma.	I am from Rome.
È fatto di legno.	It's made of wood.
di giorno	by day, in the daytime
di nuovo	again

4. **In** = In

Ho vissuto in Italia per vari anni.	I lived in Italy for several years.
Il treno partirà in orario.	The train will leave on time.
Venga in salotto.	Come into the parlor.
in quella direzione	in that direction.

5. **Fino a** = Up to, Until

fino a Milano	up to (as far as) Milano
Io sono salito fino al quinto piano.	I walked up to the fifth floor.

6. **Verso** = Towards

Ella camminava verso il parco.	She was walking toward (in the direction of) the park.
Comincio a piovere verso notte.	It started to rain towards night.

7. **Da** = From, Since.

da Napoli a Capri	from Naples to Capri
da quando lo vidi	since I saw him, since the time I saw him.

8. **Sopra** = On, or Above

sopra la tavola	above the table
Ella aveva un tetto sopra la testa.	She had a roof above her head.

9. **Per** = For, Through, In place of

L'ho comprato per un dollaro.	I bought it for a dollar.
Gli ho dato un dollaro per questo.	I gave him a dollar for this.

Egli mi ha dato il suo libro per il mio.	He exchanged books with me. (He gave me his book for mine.)
Noi siamo passati per Roma.	We passed through Rome.
Il treno passa per Roma.	The train passes through Rome.
Egli entrò per la porta.	He came in through the door.
Io vado per lei.	I'll go for (in place of) you.
Io sarò in viaggio per due anni.	I'll be away traveling for two years.

10. **Su** = On, On top of

La tovaglia è sulla tavola.	The tablecloth is on the table.
Ha un velo sui capelli.	She has a veil on her hair.

Other Expressions:

Perchè?	Why? What is the reason?
per ora, ora	for the time being
nella mattina	in the morning, during the morning
nel pomeriggio	during the afternoon, in the afternoon
di notte	at night
Egli cammino per la strada.	He walked along the street.
per esempio	for example
di conseguenza	consequently, as a result
in generale	in general
per quella ragione	for that reason
per ragione di	by reason of
a causa di	on account of

alla fine	finally, at last
qui intorno	around here
disposto a farlo	in favor of doing it
Per amor di Dio!	For goodness' sake! For heaven's sake!
invece di questo	instead of this

QUIZ 28

1.	*a mezzogiorno*	1.	on foot
2.	*poco a poco*	2.	one by one
3.	*a destra*	3.	I come from Rome.
4.	*all'italiana*	4.	It's made of wood.
5.	*con*	5.	by day
6.	*a piedi*	6.	again
7.	*Vengo da Roma.*	7.	on the table
8.	*È fatto di legno.*	8.	to the right
9.	*in rapporto a*	9.	in that direction
10.	*di nuovo*	10.	little by little
11.	*in quella direzione*	11.	until tomorrow
12.	*di giorno*	12.	at noon
13.	*a sinistra*	13.	since I saw him
14.	*uno a uno*	14.	in the Italian manner
15.	*fino a Milano*	15.	with
16.	*Partirò fra due giorni.*	16.	instead of
17.	*sulla tavola*	17.	to the left
18.	*fino a domani*	18.	in regard to
19.	*invece di*	19.	as far as Milano
20.	*da quando lo vidi*	20.	I'm leaving in two days.

ANSWERS

1-12; 2-10; 3-8; 4-14; 5-15; 6-1; 7-3; 8-4; 9-18; 10-6; 11-9; 12-5; 13-17; 14-2; 15-19; 16-20; 17-7; 18-11; 19-16; 20-13.

QUIZ 29

1. *per esempio*	1. I gave him a dollar for this.
2. *Il treno passa per Roma.*	2. I'll be away traveling for two years.
3. *Siamo passati per Roma.*	3. completely
4. *per ora*	4. for that reason
5. *L'ho comprato per un dollaro.*	5. around here
6. *per quella ragione*	6. For goodness' sake!
7. *Io sarò in viaggio per due anni.*	7. at last
8. *completamente*	8. for example
9. *Io gli ho dato un dollaro per questo.*	9. I'm not in favor of going.
10. *Per amor di Dio!*	10. for the time being
11. *alla fine*	11. I bought it for a dollar.
12. *Egli entrò per la porta.*	12. The train passes through Rome.
13. *qui intorno*	13. I take this instead of that.
14. *Non sono disposto ad andare.*	14. He came in through the door.
15. *Prendo questo invece di quello.*	15. We passed through Rome.

ANSWERS

1-8; 2-12; 3-15; 4-10; 5-11; 6-4; 7-2; 8-3; 9-1; 10-6; 11-7; 12-14; 13-5; 14-9; 15-13.

QUIZ 30

1. *La lettera è per lei.*	1. a book store
2. *Non serve a nulla.*	2. the lesson for tomorrow
3. *la lezione per domani*	3. in order to go there
4. *Sta per piovere.*	4. He left for Naples.
5. *Sono disposto a farlo.*	5. I'm studying to be a doctor.
6. *una libreria*	6. He's about to leave.
7. *per andare lì*	7. The letter is for you.
8. *È partito per Napoli.*	8. I'm in favor of doing it.
9. *Egli sta per partire.*	9. It's worthless.
10. *Sto studiando per diventare dottore.*	10. It's about to rain.

ANSWERS

1-7; 2-9; 3-2; 4-10; 5-8; 6-1; 7-3; 8-4; 9-6; 10-5.

LESSON 33

60. ASKING YOUR WAY

(Asking Your Way)

Scusi. Perdoni.
Excuse me. Pardon me.

Mi perdoni.
Pardon me.

Mi scusi.
Excuse me.

Qual'è il nome di questo paese?
What is the name of this town?

Quanto siamo distanti da Roma?
How far are we from Rome?

Quanti chilometri vi sono da qui a Roma?
How many kilometers from here to Rome?

È a dieci chilometri da qui.
It's ten kilometers from here.

È a venti chilometri da qui.
It's twenty kilometers from here.

Come arrivo a Roma da qui?
How do I get to Rome from here?

Segua questa strada.
Follow this road.

Può dirmi come posso arrivare a questo indirizzo?
Can you tell me how I can get to this address?

Può dirmi come posso arrivare a questo posto?
Can you tell me how I can get to this place?

Come si chiama questa strada?
What is the name of this street?

Può dirmi dov'è questa strada?
Can you tell me where this street is?

Dov'è via Pinciana?
Where is Pinciana Street?

È lontano da qui?
Is it far from here?

È vicino?
Is it near?

È il terzo caseggiato a destra.
It's the third block to the right.

Vada per questa strada.
Go this way.

Vada avanti diritto.
Go straight ahead.

Vada fino all'angolo e volti a sinistra.
Go to the corner and turn left.

Prenda la prima strada a sinistra.
Take the first street to the left.

Volti a destra.
Turn right.

Dov'è l'autorimessa?
Where is the garage?

Dov'è la Questura?
Where is the Police Station?

Dov'è il Municipio?
Where is City Hall?

Dov'è la fermata dell'autobus?
Where is the bus stop?

A quale fermata scendo?
At what stop do I get off?

Dove scendo?
Where do I get off?

Dov'è la stazione ferroviaria?
Where is the railroad station?

Dove si prende il treno per Roma?
Where do you get the train for Rome?

Da quale binario parte il treno per Roma?
From which track does the train for Rome leave?

A quale binario arriva il treno di Roma?
At which track does the Rome train arrive?

Dov'è l'ufficio informazioni?
Where is information?

Vuole darmi per favore un orario ferroviario?
Will you please let me have a timetable?

Qual'è il treno per Roma?
Which is the train for Rome?

È questo il treno per Roma?
Is this the train for Rome?

Dove si prende il treno per Roma?
Where do you get the train for Rome?

Al binario due.
On track two.

Quando parte il treno per Roma?
When does the train for Rome leave?

Il treno è appena partito.
The train just left.

Il treno sta per partire.
The train is about to leave.

Quando parte il prossimo treno?
When does the next train leave?

Dov'è lo sportello dei biglietti?
Where is the ticket window?

Mi dia un biglietto di andata per Roma.
Give me a one way ticket to Rome.

Di prima o di seconda classe?
First or second class?

Prima clase.
First class.

Quanto costa?
How much does it cost?

Cinquemila e cinquecento lire.
Five thousand and five hundred lire.

Quanto tempo ci vuole per arrivare?
How long does it take to get there?

Un po' più di un'ora.
A little more than an hour.

È occupato questo posto?
Is this seat taken?

Posso mettere la mia valigia qui?
May I put my suitcase here?

Che stazione è questa?
What station is this?

Quanto tempo ci fermiamo qui?
How long do we stop here?

Devo cambiare treno qui?
Do I change trains here?

Questo treno si ferma a Roma?
Does this train stop in Rome?

LESSON 34

61. WRITING, PHONING, TELEGRAPHING

(Writing, Phoning)

Ha una matita?
Do you have a pencil?

Ha una penna?
Do you have a pen?

Ha una carta assorbente?
Do you have a blotter?

Ha una busta?
Do you have an envelope?

Ha un francobollo?
Do you have a stamp?

Dove posso comprare un francobollo?
Where can I buy a stamp?

Ha un francobollo aereo?
Do you have an airmail stamp?

Dov'è l'ufficio postale?
Where is the post office?

Vorrei imbucare questa lettera.
I'd like to mail this letter.

Quanti francobolli occorrono per questa lettera?
How many stamps do I need on this letter?

Dov'è la cassetta postale più vicina?
Where is the nearest mailbox?

All'angolo.
On the corner.

Vorrei mandare un telegramma.
I'd like to send a telegram.

Dov'è l'ufficio telegrafico?
Where is the telegraph office?

È nell'ufficio postale.
It's in the post office.

Quanto costa un telegramma per Roma?
How much is a telegram to Rome?

In quanto tempo ci arriva?
How long does it take to get there?

C'è un telefono?
Is there a phone here?

Dove posso telefonare?
Where can I phone?

Dov'è il telefono?
Where is the telephone?

Dove è la cabina telefonica?
Where is the phone booth?

Nell'atrio dell'albergo.
In the hotel lobby.

Posso usare il suo telefono?
May I use your phone?

Sicuro! Si accomodi!
Of course! Go ahead!

Posso fare una chiamata interurbana?
May I have long distance?

Quanto costa una telefonata per Roma?
How much is a phone call to Rome?

Posso avere il numero otto, sette, cinque, otto, due?
May I have 87582?

Aspetti un momento.
Hold the wire a minute.

La linea è occupata.
The line is busy.

Centralino, lei mi ha dato il numero sbagliato.
Operator, you gave me the wrong number.

Non risponde.
There is no answer.

Posso parlare con il signor Ferri?
May I speak to Mr. Ferri?

In persona.
Speaking. (In person.)

Questo è il signor Villanova, (che parla).
This is Mr. Villanova speaking.

Parlo con il signor Ferri?
Am I speaking with Mr. Ferri?

Sono io.
Speaking.

Con chi parlo?
Who is this? (With whom am I speaking?)

Con il signor Ferri.
With Mr. Ferri.

LESSON 35

62. FAMILY AFFAIRS

(Family Affairs)

Come si chiama?
What's your name?

Mi chiamo Giovanni Ferri.
My name is John Ferri.

Come si chiama?
What's his name?

Si chiama Carlo Peretti.
His name is Charles Peretti.

Come si chiama?
What's her name?

Si chiama Maria Ferrari.
Her name is Maria Ferrari.

Come si chiamano?
What are their names?

Lui si chiama Giuseppe Riva e lei Anna Martini.
His name is Joseph Riva and her name is Anna
   Martini.

Qual'è il suo nome?
What's his first name?

Il suo nome è Carlo.
His first name is Charles.

Qual'è il suo cognome?
What is his last name?

Il suo cognome è Peretti.
His last name is Peretti.

Di dov'è lei?
Where are you from?

Io sono di Roma.
I'm from Rome.

Dov'è nato?
Where were you born?

Sono nato a Roma.
I was born in Rome.

Quanti anni ha?
How old are you?

Ho ventiquattro anni.
I'm twenty-four.

Compiro ventiquattro anni in settembre.
I'll be twenty-four in September.

Sono nato il diciannove agosto mille novecento sedici.
I was born August 19, 1916.

Quanti fratelli ha?
How many brothers do you have?

Ho due fratelli.
I have two brothers.

Il maggiore ha ventidue anni.
The older one is twenty-two.

Studia all'Università.
He is at the University.

Il minore ha quindici anni.
The younger one is fifteen.

Egli frequenta l'ultimo anno del ginnasio.
He's in his first year of high school.

Quante sorelle ha?
How many sisters do you have?

Ho una sorella.
I have one sister.

Ha nove anni.
She's nine.

Frequenta la scuola elementare.
She goes to grammar (primary) school.

Cosa fa suo padre?
What does your father do?

È avvocato.
He's a lawyer.

È architetto.
He's an architect.

È maestro.
He's a teacher.

È professore d'universita.
He's a university professor.

È dottore.
He's a doctor.

È uomo d'affari.
He's a businessman.

È agricoltore.
He's a farmer.

È un funzionario dello Stato.
He's in the government service.

È operaio.
He's a worker.

Lavora in uno stabilimento di automobili.
He works in an automobile factory.

Quando è il suo compleanno?
When is your birthday?

Il mio compleanno è fra due settimane, il ventitrè gennaio.
My birthday is in two weeks, January 23.

Ha parenti qui?
Do you have any relatives here?

Vive qui tutta la sua famiglia?
Does all your family live here?

Tutta la mia famiglia, meno i miei nonni.
All my family, except my grandparents.

Essi vivono in una tenuta vicino a Firenze.
They live in a country home near Florence.

È imparentato con il signor Villanova?
Are you related to Mr. Villanova?

È mio zio.
He's my uncle.

È mio cugino.
He's my cousin.

È imparentato con la signora Rossi?
Are you related to Mrs. Rossi?

È mia zia.
She's my aunt.

È mia cugina.
She's my cousin.

LESSON 36

63. SHOPPING

(Shopping, Meals)

1. **Quanto costa questo?**
   How much is this?

2. **Mille lire.**
   A thousand lire.

3. **È piuttosto caro. Non ha niente di più economico?**
   That's rather expensive. Haven't you anything cheaper?

4. **Della stessa qualità?**
   Of the same sort?

5. **La stessa qualita o qualche cosa di simile.**
   The same sort or something similar.

6. **C'è questo.**
   There's this.

7. **Non ha niente altro da farmi vedere?**
   Haven't you any other kind you could show me?

8. **Meno caro?**
   Less expensive?

9. **Se è possibile.**
   If (it's) possible.

10. **Forse le piace questo?**
    Perhaps you like this?

11. **Dipende dal prezzo.**
    That depends on the price.

12. **Questo costa ottocento lire.**
    This one is eight hundred lire.

13. **Mi piace più dell'altro.**
    I like it better than the other one.

14. **È più economico.**
    It's cheaper.

15. **Com'è questo? È più economico o più caro?**
    How about this? Is it cheaper or more expensive?

16. **È più caro.**
    It's more expensive.

17. **Non ha altro assortimento?**
    Haven't you anything else in stock?

18. **Spero di ricevere presto nuovi modelli.**
I'm hoping to receive some new styles soon.

19. **Fra quanto?**
How soon?

20. **Da un giorno all'altro. Puo ripassare verso la fine della settimana?**
Any day now. Can you drop in towards the end of the week?

21. **Lo faro ... Quanto costa questo?**
I'll do that ... What's the price of this?

22. **Cinquecento lire al paio.**
Five hundred lire a pair.

23. **Me ne dia una dozzina.**
Let me have a dozen.

24. **Vuole portarli con se?**
Will you take them with you? Will you take them yourself?

25. **Preferisco che me li mandi a casa.**
I'd rather have you send them.

26. **L'indirizzo è sempre lo stesso?**
Is the address still the same?

27. **È lo stesso.**
The same.

28. **Arrivederla.**
Good-by.

NOTES

Facendo delle compre = Shopping (Making Purchases.)

3. *È piuttosto caro* = That's rather expensive. *Molto caro* = Very expensive. *Economico,* or *a buon mercato* = Cheap. *Più economico* = Cheaper. *Molto economico* = Very cheap.

5. *Qualche cosa di simile* = Something (of) similar.

7. *Da farmi vedere* = To make me see. You can also use *mostrarmi*.

19. *Fra quanto?* Idiomatic expression for "How soon?" It can also be expressed by *Fra quanto tempo?* (In how much time?)

20. *Da un giorno all'altro* = From one day to the other.

21. *Lo farò.* (I will do that.) Future of the verb *fare*.

23. *Me ne dia una dozzina.* (Give me a dozen "of them.") *Dia* is the imperative of *dare*.

24. *Con se* = With yourself.

25. *Mandi* = subjunctive of *mandare*.

28. *Arrivederla* is used instead of *arrivederci* because the speaker is addressing only one person.

QUIZ 31

1. *È abbstanza* _____ (expensive).
   a. *costa*
   b. *questo*
   c. *caro*

2. *Ha nulla di più* _____ (cheap).
   a. *qualità*
   b. *prezzo*
   c. *economico*

3. *Della* _____ (same) *qualità*.
   a. *qualche cosa*
   b. *stessa*
   c. *più*

4. *Di* _____ (less) *prezzo.*
   a. *più*
   b. *meno*
   c. *stesso*

5. *Mi piace* _____ (more) *dell'altro.*
   a. *come*
   b. *più*
   c. *vale*

6. *Non* _____ (have) *maggiore assortimento?*
   a. *ha*
   b. *caro*
   c. *altro*

7. *Spero* _____ (receive) *notizie.*
   a. *scelta*
   b. *tranquillo*
   c. *ricevere*

8. *A* _____ (when)?
   a. *assortimento*
   b. *caro*
   c. *quando*

9. *Allo stesso* _____ (address)?
   a. *indirizzo*
   b. *domicilio*
   c. *spedire*

ANSWERS

1-c; 2-c; 3-b; 4-b; 5-b; 6-a; 7-c; 8-c; 9-a.

64. BREAKFAST

1. **P: Ha appetito?**
   Do you have an appetite?

2. **Sig: Sì, ho appetito.**
   I certainly have.

3. **P[1]: Cameriere! Cameriere!**
   Waiter! Waiter!

4. **C: Cosa desidera?**
   What do you wish?

5. **P: Verremmo fare colazione.**
   We'd like to have breakfast.

6. **Sig: Cosa ci può servire?**
   What can you serve us?

7. **C: Caffè con latte, tè con limone o con latte,
   cioccolata ...**
   Coffee with milk, tea with lemon or with
   milk, chocolate ...

8. **Sig: Con che lo servite?**
   What do you serve with it?

9. **C: Con panini, paste, biscotti ...**
   Rolls, pastry, biscuits ...

10. **Sig: Ha del burro?**
    Is there any butter?

11. **C: Sì signora.**
    Yes, Madam.

12. **Sig: Mi porti una tazza di caffè con latte.**
    Bring me a cup of coffee with milk.

13. **P: Anche a me. E mi porti pure due uova
    fritte.**
    The same for me. And bring me also two
    fried eggs.

14. **Sig: Cameriere, mi porti per favore un
    tovagliolo.**
    Waiter, would you please bring me a
    napkin?

[1]"P" represents Mr. Paoli. "Sig" stands for *Signora* (his wife),
and "C" for *Cameriere* (Waiter).

15. **P: Per me, una forchetta.**
    And a fork for me.

16. **Sig: Per favore ci porti ancora un pò di zucchero.**
    Please bring us a little more sugar.

17. **P: E poi ci porti il conto... Ecco qui, cameriere... tenga il resto.**
    And then let's have a check... Here you are, waiter... keep the change.

18. **C: Molte grazie, signore.**
    Thank you, sir.

NOTES

Colazione (Breakfast)

La colazione is called *la prima colazione* to distinguish it from *la seconda colazione* (lunch). *Il pranzo* = dinner. *La cena* = supper.

1. The subject pronoun is not necessarily used when the meaning of the sentence is obvious.

2. *Ho appetito* = I have appetite.

4. *Che* is omitted. The sentence is really: *Che cosa desidera?*

5. *Vorremmo,* condit. of *volere* (because it is a polite form).

9. *Panini* = rolls. *Panino imbottito* = sandwich (stuffed roll).

10. *Ha del burro?* = Have you some of the butter?
 del (di il) burro

13. *Un uovo* = an egg. *Uova* = eggs. (Note the irregular plural.) *Uova con pancetta* = bacon and
 eggs. *Uova alla cocca* = soft-boiled eggs ("in
 the shell"). *Uova sode* = hard-boiled eggs.
 Uova strapazzate = scrambled eggs.

17. *Tenga,* imperative of *tenere* (polite form). *Il
 resto* = the rest, the change (as a tip). *Spiccioli*
 = change, small money.

QUIZ 32

1. _____ (We want) *fare colazione.*
 a. *Desideriamo*
 b. *Mangiare*
 c. *Appetito*

2. _____ (Is there) *del burro?*
 a. *Servire*
 b. *C'è*
 c. *Potrebbe?*

3. *Mi dia lo* _____ (same).
 a. *molto*
 b. *stesso*
 c. *spero*

4. *Chi va a* _____ (eat)?
 a. *servire*
 b. *poco*
 c. *mangiare*

5. *Io mangio molto* _____ (little).
   a. *vado*
   b. *questo*
   c. *poco*

6. *Per favore* _____ (bring me) *un tovagliolo.*
   a. *costume*
   b. *mi porti*
   c. *dirà*

7. _____ (Afterwards) *ci porti il conto.*
   a. *Favore*
   b. *Forchetta*
   c. *Dopo*

ANSWERS

1-a; 2-b; 3-b; 4-c; 5-c; 6-b; 7-c.

65. A SAMPLE MENU

Lista	Menu
Antipasto	Hors d'oeuvres
Minestrone	Vegetable soup
Passato di piselli	Pea soup
Frittata al prosciutto	Ham omelet
Pollo arrosto (pollo alla diavola)	Roast chicken (devil-style chicken)
Abbacchio (alla romana)	Roast lamb (Roman-style)
Bistecca con patate fritte	Steak with French-fried potatoes

Insalata verde con pomodori	Green (fresh) salad with tomatoes
Formaggio e frutta	Cheese and fruit
Caffè	Coffee

LESSON 37

66. APARTMENT HUNTING

(Apartment Hunting)

1. **Sono venuta a vedere l'appartamento.**
   I've come to see the apartment.
2. **Quale? Quale dei due?**
   Which one? Which of the two?
3. **Quello che è da affittare.**
   The one which is for rent.
4. **Ce ne sono due.**
   There are two.
5. **Me li può descrivere?**
   Can you describe them?
6. **Quello al quinto piano non è ammobiliato.**
   The one on the fifth floor is unfurnished.
7. **E quell'altro?**
   And the other one?
8. **L'altro al secondo piano è ammobiliato.**
   The one of the second floor is furnished.
9. **Quante camere ci sono?**
   How many rooms are there?
10. **Quello al quinto piano è di quattro camere, cucina e bagno.**
    The one on the fifth floor has four rooms, kitchen and bath.
11. **Dà sulla strada?**
    Does it face the street?
12. **No, dà sul cortile.**
    No, it faces the court.

13. **E quello al secondo piano?**
    And the one on the second floor?

14. **Quello al secondo piano ha una camera da letto, un salotto e una camera da pranzo.**
    The one on the second floor has a bedroom, a living room and a dining room.

15. **Dà anch' esso sul cortile?**
    Does it also face the court?

16. **No, dà sulla strada.**
    No, it faces the street.

17. **Quanto è la pigione?**
    How much is the rent?

18. **Il più grande costa trentotto mila lire al mese, più luce e gas.**
    The larger one is 38,000 lire a month, plus light and gas.

19. **E quello ammobiliato?**
    And the furnished one?

20. **Quello costa quarantacinque mila lire al mese, tutto incluso.**
    That one costs 45,000 lire a month, everything included.

21. **Come ammobiliato? In che condizioni e la mobilia?**
    How is it furnished? In what condition is the furniture?

22. **Il mobilio è moderno ed è in ottime condizioni.**
    It's modern furniture and it's in excellent condition.

23. **La biancheria e i piatti sono inclusi?**
    Are linen and silverware (dishes) included?

24. **Troverà tutto quello che le occorre, perfino un servizio completo di stroviglie.**
    You'll find everything you need, even a complete set of kitchen utensils.

25. **Bisogna firmare un contratto lungo?**
    Does one have to sign a long lease?

26. **Per questo dovrà vedere l'amministratore.**
You'll have to see the renting agent for that.

27. **Quali sono le condizioni?**
What are the terms?

28. **Un mese anticipato e uno di deposito.**
One month's rent in advance and another month's rent as a deposit.

29. **È tutto?**
Is that all?

30. **Naturalmente, dovrà dare le sue referenze.**
Of course you'll have to give references.

31. **A proposito, c'è l'ascensore?**
By the way, is there an elevator?

32. **No, non c'è ascensore.**
No, there isn't any elevator.

33. **Che peccato!**
That's too bad! (What a sin!)

34. **A parte questo, la casa è molto moderna.**
Aside from that, the house is very modern.

35. **Che cosa vuol dire?**
What do you mean?

36. **C'è riscaldamento centrale e una scala di servizio.**
There's central heating and a back stairway (service stairway).

37. **C'è acqua calda?**
Is there any hot water?

38. **Naturalmente. Le camere da bagno sono state rimodernate di recente.**
Of course. The bathrooms were recently remodeled.

39. **Ah, mi dimenticavo . . . ci sono le camere per la servitù?**
Oh, I forgot . . . are there servants' rooms?

40. **Si, e anche molto belle.**
Yes, (and) very good ones too (very beautiful).

41. **Si possono vedere gli appartamenti?**
Can one see the apartments?

42. **Soltanto la mattina.**
Only in the morning.

43. **Va bene. Verrò domani mattina. Molte grazie.**
Very well. I'll come tomorrow morning. Thanks a lot.

44. **Di nulla. S'immagini. Felice d'averla servita.**
Not at all. Don't mention it. Glad to be able to help you.

NOTES

In Cerca di un Appartamento (In Search of an Apartment)

1. *A* = in order to.

4. *ce* is used instead of *ci*, because *ci, mi, ti, vi,* become *ce, me, te, ve* before *ne.*

5. *me li:* as in 4.

9. *ci sono* = there are.

11. Idiomatic expression. *Dare* = to give, but also "to face."

13. The first floor in Italy is called *painterreno;* what we call the "second floor" in America is the *primo piano* in Italy.

21. *Il mobile* = piece of furniture. *I mobili* = the furniture *(pl.)*
La mobilia, il mobilio = furniture *(sing.)*

22. *Ottime:* superlative of *buone (fem, pl.).*

23. *I piatti* includes dishes and silverware. *Il piatto da portata* = the serving dish. *L'argenteria* = the silverware.

24. *Stoviglie* includes everything pertaining to the kitchen.
26. *L'amministratore* = the manager.
30. Note article in front of *sue (possessive)*.
31. The definite article is often used in Italian where the indefinite is used in English.
33. *Che peccato!* = What a sin!
34. This apart.
35. *Vuol:* the final *e (vuole)* of verb forms is often dropped in speaking.
38. *sono state rimodernate* = have been remodeled.
39. "I forgot myself." *Dimenticare* is used reflexively. *la donna di servizio* = the maid.
41. *Si possono vedere* = Is it possible to see the apartments. (Impersonal use of verb: "Can one see_____"
44. *S'immagini* = Imagine. A polite way to express "Don't mention it." Also: *Ma le pare.*

QUIZ 33

1. _____ (I come) *per vedere l'appartamento.*
   a. *Vengo*
   b. *Sono*
   c. *Voglio*
2. *Quello* _____ (for) *affittare.*
   a. *in*
   b. *per*
   c. *da*
3. _____ (There are) *due.*
   a. *C'è*
   b. *Ce ne sono*
   c. *Sono*
4. *È* _____ (without) *mobili.*
   a. *con*
   b. *senza*
   c. *tra*

5. _____ (How much) *è la pigione?*
   a. *Quando*
   b. *Quanto*
   c. *Troppo*

6. _____ (Does it face) *sulla strada?*
   a. *Guarda*
   b. *Faccia*
   c. *Dà*

7. *Dà* _____ (also) *sul giardino?*
   a. *altro*
   b. *anche*
   c. *poi*

8. _____ (It costs) *sei mila lire.*
   a. *Costa*
   b. *Quanto*
   c. *Viene*

9. *Bisogna* _____ (sign) *un contratto?*
   a. *scrivere*
   b. *segnare*
   c. *firmare*

10. *La casa è* _____ (very) *moderna.*
   a. *molto*
   b. *tanto*
   c. *male*

ANSWERS

1-a; 2-c; 3-b; 4-b; 5-b; 6-c; 7-b; 8-a; 9-c; 10-a.

67. SOME COMMON VERBS

Avere = to have

io ho	I have
tu hai	you have
egli ha	he has
noi abbiamo	we have
voi avete	you have
essi hanno	they have

a. *Avere* also means "to have" in the sense of "to possess."

Io ho questo.	I have this. I've got this.
Io non ho nulla.	I don't have anything.
Lo ha lei?	Do you have it?
Io non l'ho.	I don't have it.
Io ho tempo.	I have time.
Io non ho denaro.	I haven't any money.
Io non ho tempo.	I haven't any time.
Egli non ha amici.	He hasn't any friends.
Io ho fame.	I'm hungry.
Io ho sete.	I'm thirsty.
Io ho sonno.	I'm sleepy.
Io ho freddo.	I'm cold.
Io ho caldo.	I'm warm.
Io ho ragione.	I'm right.
Egli non ha ragione.	He is not right.
Essi non hanno ragione.	They're wrong.
Ha lei degli amici a Roma?	Do you have (any) friends in Rome?
Io non ho amici a Roma.	I don't have any friends in Rome.
Ha (lei) una sigaretta?	Do you have a cigarette?
Io non ho sigarette.	I don't have any cigarettes.

Ha (lei) un fiammifero?	Do you have a light (a match)?
Non ho fiammiferi.	I don't have any matches.
Io ho vent'anni.	I'm twenty.
(Io) ho mal di testa.	I have a headache.
(Io) ho mal di denti.	I have a toothache.
Che cosa hai?	What's the matter with you?
Non ho nulla.	Nothing's the matter with me.
Quanto denaro ha?	How much money do you have?
Io non ho denaro (affatto).	I haven't any money (at all).
Io ho molto da fare.	I have a lot to do.

b. Do I have it?

L'ho (Io ho) io?	Do I have it?
L'hai tu?	Do you have it? *(fam.)*
L'ha lei?	Do you have it? *(polite)*
L'ha egli?	Does he have it?
L'abbiamo noi?	Do we have it?
L'avete voi?	Do you have it? *(fam. pl.)*
L'hanno loro?	{ Do they have it? { Do you have it? *(polite pl.)*

c. Don't I have it?

Non l'ho (Io ho) io?	Don't I have it?
Non l'hai tu?	Don't you have it? *(fam.)*
Non l'ha lei?	Don't you have it? *(polite)*
Non l'ha egli?	Doesn't he have it?
Non l' abbiamo noi?	Don't we have it?

Non l' avete voi?   Don't you have it?
                     (fam. pl.)

Non l' hanno loro?   { Don't they have it?
                     { Don't you have it?
                     (polite pl.)

QUIZ 34

1. *Non ho denaro.*
2. *Non ho nulla.*
3. *Egli non ha ragione.*
4. *Ho sonno.*
5. *L'ha egli.*
6. *Non l'ho.*

7. *Ho fame.*
8. *Ho freddo.*
9. *Ho venti'anni.*
10. *Non l'ha lei?*
11. *Io devo andare.*

12. *Ho caldo.*
13. *Ho sete.*
14. *Ho mal di testa.*
15. *Ho molto da fare.*

1. I have a headache.
2. Don't you have it?
3. I don't have it.

4. I'm cold.
5. I'm warm.
6. I don't have any money.

7. Does he have it?
8. He's not right.
9. I'm thirsty.
10. I have a lot to do.
11. I don't have anything.

12. I'm sleepy.
13. I'm hungry.
14. I have to leave.
15. I'm twenty years old.

ANSWERS

1-6; 2-11; 3-8; 4-12; 5-7; 6-3; 7-13; 8-4; 9-15; 10-2; 11-14; 12-5; 13-9; 14-1; 15-10.

LESSON 38

68. I AM A STRANGER

(Sightseeing)

1. **Mi scusi.**
   Pardon me.
2. **In che cosa posso servirla?**
   What can I do for you?
3. **Mi potrebbe dare alcune informazioni?**
   Could you give me some information?
4. **Con molto piacere.**
   Gladly. (With much pleasure.)
5. **Io non conosco questa città e non mi posso orientare.**
   I don't know this town and I can't find my way around.
6. **Bene, è abbastanza semplice.**
   Well, it's quite simple.
7. **Come vede, io sono straniera.**
   As you see, I'm a stranger (here).
8. **In questo caso le mostrerò la città.**
   In that case I'll show you the town.
9. **La ringrazierò moltissimo. Lo apprezzerò molto.**
   I'd be very grateful to you. I'd appreciate that a lot.
10. **Vede quel gran palazzo all'angolo?**
    Do you see that large building on the corner?
11. **Quello con la bandiera?**
    The one with the flag?
12. **Esattamente. Quello è la Posta Centrale. Di fronte a desso dall'altro lato della strada...**

That's right. (Exactly.) That's the main Post Office. Opposite it, on the other side of the street . . .

13. **Dove?**
Where?

14. **Da quella parte. Vede quell'altro palazzo con degli archi?**
Over there. Do you see that other building with arches?

15. **Oh, sì, adesso lo vedo.**
Oh, yes, now I see.

16. **Quella è la Galleria Colonna.**
That's the Colonna Gallery.

17. **La vedo. . . . A proposito, qual'è il nome di questa piazza?**
I see it. . . . By the way, what's the name of this square?

18. **Piazza San Silvestro.**
Saint Silvester Square.

19. **Dov'è la Questura?**
Where is the Police Station?

20. **In fondo a quella strada, a destra.**
At the end of the street, to the right.

21. **E se non lo trovo?**
What if I miss it? (If I don't find it?)

22. **Non si preoccupi. È un gran polazzo grigio, con due guardie di fronte all'entrata. Vede quel negozio?**
Don't worry. It's a big, gray building with two guards in front of the entrance. You see that store?

23. **Quale negozio? Quello a sinistra?**
Which store? The one on the left?

24. **Esattamente. Quello che ha quel grosso globo di vetro verde in vetrina.**
Right. The one with the large green globe (of glass) in the window.

25. **È una barbieria?**
It's a barber-shop?

26. **No, è una farmacia. Al lato del negozio c'è la casa del dottore. Il suo nome è sulla porta.**
No, it's a pharmacy. The doctor lives right next door. (Next to the store is the doctor's house.) His name is on the door.

27. **Ha l'ufficio nella stessa casa in cui abita?**
Does he have his office there as well? (Does he have his office in the same house in which he lives?)

28. **Sì, ma tutte le mattine va all'ospedale.**
Yes, but he spends every morning at the hospital.

29. **Dov'è l'ospedale?**
Where is the hospital?

30. **Per raggiungere l'ospedale, lei deve camminare per il corso Umberto, verso piazza del Popolo. All penultima strada a sinistra si trova via San Giacomo, e l'Ospedale San Giacomo è là.**
To reach the hospital, you must take the Umberto Corso (Avenue), towards Popolo Square. A block before reaching the Square, you will come to Saint Giacomo (James) Street, and there you'll find the Saint Giacomo hospital.

31. **Come posso ritornare al mio albergo?**
How can I get back to my hotel?

32. **Vada per questa strada. Lo vede là, dopo il . . .**
Go this way. You see it there, next to the . . .

33. **...cinema? Non è così?**
...movies? That's right, isn't it? (Isn't it so?)

34. **Esatto.**
Yes. (Exact.)

35. **Oro ho capito.**
Now I understand.

36. **Perchè non si compra una guida?**
Why don't you buy yourself a guidebook?

37. **Non è una cattiva idea. Dove posso comprarla?**
That's not a bad idea. Where can I buy one?

38. **Alla stazione ferroviaria, oppure in qualsiasi chiosco di giornali.**
At the station, or at any newspaper stand.

39. **È lontana da qui la stazione?**
Is the station far from here?

40. **La stazione si trova in piazza Cinquecento.**
The station is in Cinquecento (Five Hundred) Square.

41. **Dove si trova un chiosco di giornali qui vicino?**
Where's there a newspaper stand near here?

42. **Ce n'è uno all'angolo.**
There's one on the corner.

43. **La ringrazio molto.**
Thank you very much. (I thank you very much.)

44. **Non c'è di che. Sono molto lieto di esserle stato utile.**
Not at all. I'm very glad to have been of help to you. (I'm very glad to have been useful to you.)

45. **Sono stata molto fortunata di averla incontrata. Lei conosce questa citta molto bene.**
I was certainly lucky to meet you. You really know this town very well.

46. **Non si sorprenda. Io sono il Sindaco.**
It's not surprising. (Don't be surprised.) I'm the mayor.

NOTES

Sono straniero. (I'm a stranger.)

2. *In che cosa posso servirla?* = In what thing can I serve you?

3. *Potrebbe:* condit. of *potere.*

5. *Orientarsi* = to orient oneself.

6. *Abbastanza* = enough.

9. *Apprezzerò:* future of *apprezzare.*

10. *Gran:* abbreviated form of *grande.*

12. *La posta centrale* = main post office. *La posta* = the mail.

14. *Palazzo* = building; also *edificio. Il palazzo* can also be "a palace."

24. In Italy, pharmacies usually have a green globe, or a big vase, in the window.

25. *La barbierìa* = the barber shop; *un barbière* = a barber; can also be called *parrucchiere.*

30. *La penultima strada* = the street before the last. In Italy, people count by streets, not by blocks. There is actually no real word for block. *Caseggiato* is a group of buildings which might sometimes correspond to an American block.

33. *Cinema* is really the "Movie Theatre." The movie (film) is called *la pellicola.*

35. *Ho capito* = I have understood. This is past tense, but this expression is often used instead of *capisco* with the same meaning.

37. *Cattiva* = bad, meaning literally "ugly." *Brutto* is also often used with the meaning of "bad." *Che brutta idea!* = What a bad idea!

44. *Non c'è di che.* (There is nothing about it . . . you are welcome.) A polite formula to use in answer to *grazie* (thank you). Another currently used expression is *prego*.
   Sono molto lieto di esserle stato utile. (I am very glad to have been of help to you.) A polite expression.

46. *Non si sorprenda.* = Don't surprise yourself.

QUIZ 35

1. *È molto _____ (simple).*
   a. *poco*
   b. *semplice*
   c. *città*

2. *Le farò vedere la _____ (city).*
   a. *caso*
   b. *città*
   c. *orientare*

3. *Questo grande palazzo all'_____ (corner).*
   a. *angolo*
   b. *via*
   c. *ufficio postale*

4. *Questo è l'_____ (post office).*
   a. *via*
   b. *ufficio postale*
   c. *altro*

5. *Vede questo _____ (store)?*
   a. *destra*
   b. *negozio*
   c. *barbiere*

6. *Nella casa vicina c'è un _____ (doctor).*
   a. *dottore*
   b. *farmacia*
   c. *nome*

7. *Il suo nome è sulla* _____ (door).
   a. *stesso*
   b. *porta*
   c. *clinica*

8. *Ha l'ufficio nells stessa* _____ (house) *in cui vive?*
   a. *dopo*
   b. *lato*
   c. *casa*

9. *Un poco* _____ (before) *di arrivare alla strada principale.*
   a. *dopo*
   b. *prima*
   c. *passata*

10. *Dove posso* _____ (buy) *questo?*
    a. *comprare*
    b. *guida*
    c. *stazione*

ANSWERS

1-b; 2-b; 3-a; 4-b; 5-b; 6-a; 7-b; 8-c; 9-b; 10-a.

LESSON 39

69. GREETING AN OLD FRIEND

(Conversation)

1. **P: Oh, eccoti qui! Come stai?**
   Oh, there you are! How are you?

2. **L[1]: E tu come stai?**
   How are you?

3. **P: Non sei troppo stanco del tuo viaggio?**
   Not too tired from your trip?

[1]"L" represents Lanzi, a friend of Mr. Paoli's.

4. **L: Niente affatto!**
Not at all!

5. **P: Desidero presentarti a mia moglie.**
I'd like you to meet my wife.

6. **L: Con molto piacere.**
I'd be very happy to.

7. **P: Cara, ti presento Giovanni Lanzi.**
This is Giovanni Lanzi, dear.

8. **L: Molto felice di conoscerla, signora.**
I'm very happy to know you.

9. **Sig: Molto piacere.**
Glad to know you.

10. **L: E'stato un vero piacere per me il rive-
derti.**
It's really very good to see you again.

11. **P: Anche per me. Tu non sei cambiato
affatto.**
I feel the same way about it. (For me, too.)
You haven't changed a bit.

12. **L: E neanche tu.**
Neither have you.

13. **Sig: Cosa pensa la signora Lanzi degli Stati
Uniti?**
How does Mrs. Lanzi like the United
States?

14. **L: Le piacciono moltissimo.**
She likes it a lot.

15. **Sig: Deve essere molto diverso da Roma,
no?**
It must be very different from Rome,
isn't it?

16. **L: Negli Stati Uniti, decisamente, ci sono
molte cose strane!**
There certainly are lots of very curious
things in the United States.

17. **Sig: Per esempio?**
    For example?

18. **L: Per esempio, non mi sarebbe mai venuto in mente di far colazione in una farmacia!**
    For example, it certainly would never have come to my mind to have lunch in a pharmacy!

19. **P: Ma vuoi scherzare!**
    You are joking!

20. **L: Niente affatto. Sto dicendo sul serio.**
    Not at all. I'm very serious.

21. **Sig: Suvvia, ci racconti. Lei vuol dire che si può fare colazione . . . in una farmacia?**
    Come, tell us about it. You mean one can have lunch . . . in a pharmacy?

22. **L: Certamente, signora. Lei puo anche ordinare una bistecca.**
    Naturally, madam. You can even have a steak.

23. **P: In una farmacia?**
    In a pharmacy?

24. **L: Sì, in una farmacia, e con un ottimo gelato per dolce.**
    Yes, in a pharmacy, and with excellent ice cream for dessert.

25. **Sig: Ma l'odore della farmacia, non disturba?**
    But the smell of the pharmacy, doesn't that bother you?

26. **L: Non c'è nessun odore nelle nostre . . .**
    There isn't any smell in our . . .

27. **P: Farmacie?**
    Pharmacies?

28. **L: In America, non le chiamano farmacie, ma drugstores.**
In America, they don't call them pharmacies, but drugstores.

29. **P: Oh...qui sta l'inganno! Le chiamano con nomi differenti!**
Oh...that's the trick! They give them a different name!

30. **Sig: Ma come può questo cambiare le cose?**
But how does that change things?

31. **P: Allora, non è più una farmacia!**
Then it's no longer a pharmacy!

32. **L: Nel "drugstore" si vendono anche molte altre cose, come giocattoli, francobolli, sigarette, caramelle...**
You also find other things in a drugstore: toys, stamps, cigarettes, candy...

33. **P: Questo è veramente buffo!**
That's really very funny!

34. **L: ...libri, carta da scrivere, utensili da cucina, articoli da toletta, e altro.**
...books, stationery, cooking utensils, toilet articles, and what-have-you.

35. **P: Allora, è un bazar?**
It's a bazaar, then?

36. **L: No, mio caro, è sempre un "drugstore!"**
No, my dear, it's (still) a drugstore!

NOTES

Salutando un vecchio amico. (Greeting an old friend.)

2. The *tu (fam.)* pronoun is used because two old friends are speaking.

4. *Niente affatto* = nothing done *(niente a-fatto:* from *fare).*

18. *Sarebbe venuto* = It would have come. *(Venuto:* past part. of *venire.* Double negation because the sentence begins with *non.)*

19. *Scherzare* = to joke. *Lo scherzo* = the joke. Other words are: *la barzelletta, la freddura.*

20. *Sul serio* = on the serious side, or seriously.

21. *Suvvia* = Come on! The word is really composed of two expressions meaning "come on": *su* and *via.* Here the two words are linked by an extra *v.*

24. *Ottimo* is really the superlative of *buono,* meaning "excellent."

26. Another example of the double negation often used in Italian.

29. *L'inganno* is also "deceit" from the verb *ingannare* (to deceive).

QUIZ 36

1. _____ (How) *stai?*
   a. *Qui*
   b. *Dove*
   c. *Come*

2. *Non sei troppo* _____ (tired) *dal tuo viaggio?*
   a. *affatto*
   b. *felice*
   c. *stanco*

3. *Desidero presentarti a mia* _____ (wife).
   a. *moglie*
   b. *molto*
   c. *piacere*

4. *È stato un vero* _____ (pleasure) *per me.*
   a. *cambiato*
   b. *piacere*
   c. *conoscere*

5. *Le piacciono* _____ (a lot).
   a. *moltissimo*
   b. *molto*
   c. *diverso*

6. *Ci sono molte* _____ (things) *strane!*
   a. *vero*
   b. *decisamente*
   c. *cose*

7. *Sto dicendo sul* _____ (serious).
   a. *serio*
   b. *scherzare*
   c. *venuto*

8. *Non le* _____ (call) *famarcie.*
   a. *chiamano*
   b. *inganno*
   c. *cambiare*

9. _____ (Then) *è un bazar?*
   a. *Allora*
   b. *Anche*
   c. *Sempre*

10. *Nel "drugstore" si vendono* _____ (stamps).
    a. *giocattoli*
    b. *francobolli*
    c. *caramelle*

ANSWERS

1-c; 2-c; 3-a; 4-b; 5-a; 6-c; 7-a; 8-a; 9-a; 10-b.

70. SOME IMPORTANT IRREGULAR VERBS

1. *Potere* = to be able

PRESENT	PAST	FUTURE	PAST PART.
io posso	io potei	io potrò	potuto
tu puoi	tu potesti	tu potrai	
egli può	egli potè	egli potrà	
lei può	lei potè	lei potrà	
noi possiamo	noi potemmo	noi potremo	
voi potete	voi poteste	voi potrete	
essi possono	essi poterono	essi potranno	
loro possono	loro poterono	loro potranno	

Posso?	May I? Can I? Do I have the permission to?
Dove posso mandare un telegramma?	Where can I send a telegram?
Potrai venire questa sera?	Will you be able to come tonight?

2. *Dovere* = to have to

PRESENT	PAST	FUTURE	PAST PART.
io devo	io dovei	io dovrò	dovuto
tu devi	tu dovesti	tu dovrai	
egli deve	egli dovè	egli dovrà	
noi dobbiamo	noi dovemmo	noi dovremo	
voi dovete	voi doveste	voi dovrete	
essi devono	essi doverono	essi devranno	

Devo farlo.	I must do it.
Io ti devo cinque dollari.	I owe you five dollars.
Dovrei andarci. (conditional)	I ought to go there.

3. *Volere* = to want.

PRESENT	PAST	FUTURE	PAST PART.
io voglio	io volli	io vorrò	voluto
tu vuoi	tu volesti	tu vorrai	
egli vuole	egli volle	egli vorrà	
noi vogliamo	noi volemmo	noi vorremo	
voi volete	voi voleste	voi vorrete	
essi vogliono	essi vollero	essi vorranno	

Voler bene a qualcuno.	To like someone.
Voglio farlo.	I wish to do it.
Vorrei finire.	I would like to finish.
(conditional)	

4. *Sapere* = to know

PRESENT	PAST	FUTURE	PAST PART.
io so	io seppi	io saprò	saputo
tu sai	tu sapesti	tu saprai	
egli sa	egli seppe	egli saprà	
noi sappiamo	noi sapemmo	noi sapremo	
voi sapete	voi sapeste	voi saprete	
essi sanno	essi seppero	essi sapranno	

Lo so che è vero.	I know it's true.
Hai saputo la notizia?	Did you hear the news?
Essi lo sapranno in tempo.	They'll find out in time.

5. *Andare* = to go

PRESENT	PAST	FUTURE	PAST PART.
io vado	io andai	io andrò	andato
tu vai	tu andasti	tu andrai	
egli va	egli andò	egli andrà	
noi andiamo	noi andammo	noi andremo	
voi andate	voi andaste	voi andrete	
essi vanno	essi andarono	essi andranno	

Sono andato a piedi.	I walked (I went on foot).
Andremo insieme.	We'll go together.
Vada presto! (imperative)	Go quickly!

6. *Venire* = to come

PRESENT	PAST	FUTURE	PAST PART.
io vengo	*io venni*	*io verrò*	*venuto*
tu vieni	*tu venisti*	*tu verrai*	
egli viene	*egli venne*	*egli verrà*	
noi veniamo	*noi venimmo*	*noi verremo*	
voi venite	*vi veniste*	*voi verrete*	
essi vengono	*essi vennero*	*essi verranno*	

Vieni con me, non è vero?	You're coming with me, aren't you?
Viene sempre da me.	He always comes to my house.
Quando verrà ella?	When will she come?
Vengono spesso in città.	They often come to the city.
Venga domani verso le tre. (imperative)	Come tomorrow at about three.

LESSON 40

71. BRIGHTER ITALIAN

(Brighter Italian)

An Optimist

Il capo di una importante casa commerciale, leggendo una richiesta di lavoro, si meraviglia moltissimo nel notare che il richiedente, pur non avendo esperienza, domanda uno stipendio eccessivo.

—Non le sembra di richiedere uno stipendio troppo alto, considerando la sua poca esperienza in merito?

—Tutt'altro, risponde il richiedente, assumere un lavoro del quale non si sa assolutamente nulla, è cosa molto più difficile, e dovrebbe essere pagata molto meglio.

The head of an important firm, looking at an application, is astonished when he notices that the applicant, though lacking experience, asks for an excessive salary.

Rather puzzled, he asks him: "Doesn't it seem to you that you are asking for an excessive salary, considering the little experience you have?"

"On the contrary," replies the applicant. "Work performed by one who knows nothing about it is harder and should be better paid."

NOTES

1. *Si meraviglia moltissimo* = Is very much amazed. *Meravigliarsi:* to wonder, to be astonished, to be surprised.

2. *Nel* is a contraction for *in il*.

3. *Pur* = although. (Always followed by the participle.)

4. *Non le sembra di richiedere* = Does it not seem to you to ask.
   Le sembra = It seems to you.
   Mi sembra = It seems to me.
   Ci sembra = It seems to us.

5. *tutt'altro* = everything else, on the contrary.

6. *dovrebbe:* condit. of *dovere* (*dovrebbe* = it should be).

UNA PERDITA DI POCA IMPORTANZA
(A Minor Loss)

—Signora, per favore, mi dia una copia del "Messaggero." Non ho spiccioli. Può cambiarmi queste mille lire?

—Può pagare domani—risponde la giornalaia.

—E se morissi questa notte?

—Oh, non sarebbe davvero una grande perdita.

"Madam, please give me a copy of the 'Messenger.' I haven't any change. Could you change this bill of one thousand lire for me?"

"You can pay for it tomorrow," says the woman selling the newspaper.

"What if I should die tonight?"

"Oh, it wouldn't be a very great loss."

NOTES

1. *Spiccioli* = change, "little money."

2. *E se morissi:* if I should die (past subjunctive of *morire*).

3. *Sarebbe:* condit. of "to be" (It would [not] be).

UNA LEZIONE DI ETICHETTA
(A Lesson in Etiquette)

Pietro e Giovanni vanno a mangiare in un ristorante. Entrambi ordinano una bistecca. Il cameriere li serve poco dopo. Pietro afferra subito la bistecca più grande. Giovanni, seccato, gli dice:

—Come sei maleducato! Ti servi per primo e ti prendi anche il pezzo più grande.

Pietro gli risponde:

—Se tu fossi stato al mio posto, quale pezzo avresti scelto?

—Il più piccolo, naturalmente.

—E allora, perchè ti lamenti? Non lo hai il più piccolo?

Peter and John go to a restaurant to eat. They both ask for steak. The waiter brings the steaks to them shortly afterwards. Peter grabs the larger steak. John says to him angrily:

"What bad manners you have! You helped yourself first and you took the larger piece."

Peter answers:

"If you had been in my place, which piece would you have taken?

"The smaller, of course."

"Then what are you complaining about? You have it, haven't you?"

NOTES

1. *Entrambi* = both of them; also *tutti e due*.

2. *Sei:* familiar form of the present "to be." (Pietro and Giovanni are friends.)

3. *Se tu fossi stato* = If you had been. (The pluperfect subjunctive is used in this case to indicate a condition contrary to fact.)

4. *Avresti scelto:* past condit. of *scegliere;* expresses the second part of the condit. sentence.
Se io fossi stato in quel ristorante, avrei ordinato pollo arrosto.
If I had been in that restaurant, I would have ordered roast chicken.

5. *Lamenti* = you lament yourself. *Lamentarsi:* reflexive verb meaning "to lament," "to complain."

72. IMPORTANT SIGNS

Signori o Uomini	Men
Signore o Donne	Women
Gabinetto	Toilet
Chiuso	Closed
Aperto	Open
Proibito fumare ⎫	No Smoking
Vietato fumare ⎬	
Vietato l'ingresso	No Admittance
Bussare	Knock
Suonare il campanello	Ring
Strada privata	Private street
Per informazioni rivolgersi qui	Inquire Within
Alt! ⎫	Stop!
Stop! ⎬	
Fermo! ⎭	
Via libera!	Go!
Attenzione!	Look out!
Pericolo	Danger
Rallentare	Go slow
Svolta obbligata	Detour
Attenzione	Cauton (Look out)
Mantenere la destra	Keep to the right

Ponte	Bridge
Divieto di sosta	No parking
Ufficio controllo	Check room
Cambio	Money Exchanged
Informazioni	Information
Sala d'aspetto	Waiting Room
Vietato sporgesi (dalla finestra)	Don't lean out (of the window)
Treno merci	Freight Car
Binario ferroviario	Railroad track
Direttissimo	Express
Accelerato (omnibus)	Local
Fermata	Stop (bus, streetcar, etc.)
Vietata l'affissione	Post No Bills
In riparazione	Under Repair
Entrata	Entrance
Uscita	Exit
Camere ammobiliate	Furnished Rooms
Appartamenti	Apartments
Pittura fresca	Wet Paint
Incrocio	Crossroads
Macelleria	Butcher (Butcher's Shop)
Panificio	Bakery
Latteria	Dairy
Sartoria	Tailor Shop (also for women)
Calzoleria	Shoe store
Barbiere	Barber Shop (barber)
Salumeria	Grocer
Farmacia	Pharmacy, Drugstore
Pasticceria	Candy Store
Cartoleria	Stationery Store
Cassetta delle lettere } *Buca delle lettere*	Letter Box
Bar	Bar
Questura	Police Station

Vini	Wines
Rifornimento benzina	Gas Station
Libreria	Book Store
Municipio	City Hall
Bibite—Gelati	Drinks—Ice Cream
Acqua fredda	Cold water
Acqua calda	Hot water

QUIZ 37

1.	*Entrata*	1.	No Smoking
2.	*Svolta obbligata*	2.	Express
3.	*Vietato sporgersi (dalla finestra)*	3.	No Parking
4.	*Chiuso*	4.	Open
5.	*Aperto*	5.	Exit
6.	*Vietato fumare*	6.	Information
7.	*Espresso*	7.	Detour
8.	*Divieto di sosta*	8.	Entrance
9.	*Uscita*	9.	Closed
10.	*Informazioni*	10.	Don't lean out (of the window)

ANSWERS

1-8; 2-7; 3-10; 4-9; 5-4; 6-1; 7-2; 8-3; 9-5; 10-6.

FINAL QUIZ

If you get 100% on this Quiz, you can consider that

you have mastered the course.

1. _____ (Tell me) *dov'è la stazione.*
   a. *Mi permetta*
   b. *Mi dica*
   c. *Mi porti*

2. _____ (Can) *dirmi dov'è l'ufficio postale?*
   a. *Può*
   b. *Avere*
   c. *Costo*

3. *Dove* _____ (is) *un buon ristorante?*
   a. *fare*
   b. *c'è*
   c. *oggi*

4. _____ (Bring me) *un po' di pane.*
   a. *Conoscerla*
   b. *Mi permetta*
   c. *Mi porti*

5. _____ (I need) *di sapone.*
   a. *Ho bisogno*
   b. *Avere*
   c. *Permette*

6. _____ (I would like) *un po' più di carne.*
   a. *Mi porti*
   b. *Mi manca*
   c. *Desidero*

7. *La* _____ (I introduce) *alla mia amica.*
   a. *presento*
   b. *ho*
   c. *venga*

8. *Dove* _____ (is) *il libro?*
   a. *è*
   b. *quello*
   c. *questo*

9. *Abbia* _____ (the goodness) *di parlare lenta-mente.*
   a. *la bontà*
   b. *il piacere*
   c. *il favore*

10. _____ (Do you understand) *l'italiano?*
    a. *Comprendo*
    b. *Parla*
    c. *Comprende*

11. _____ (Go) *là.*
    a. *Vada*
    b. *Parla*
    c. *Essere*

12. _____ (Come) *subito.*
    a. *Venga*
    b. *Vado*
    c. *Andiamo*

13. *Come si* _____ (call) *lei?*
    a. *lavare*
    b. *chiama*
    c. *chiamano*

14. *Che giorno della* _____ (week) *è oggi?*
    a. *settimana*
    b. *mese*
    c. *anno*

15. *Che* _____ (time) *è?*
    a. *ora*
    b. *adesso*
    c. *ho*

16. *Non* _____ (I have) *sigarette.*
    a. *tempo*
    b. *ho*
    c. *avere*

17. _____ (Do you want) *della frutta?*
    a. *Potrebbe*
    b. *Ha lei*
    c. *Desidera*

18. _____ (Allow me) *di presentarla al mio amico.*
    a. *Dare*
    b. *Mi permetta*
    c. *Mi porti*

19. _____ (I wish) *scrivere una lettera.*
    a. *Desidera*
    b. *Desidero*
    c. *Mi permetta*

20. *Quanto* _____ (costs) *un telegramma per Milano?*
    a. *costa*
    b. *costare*
    c. *conto*

21. *Desideriamo fare* _____ (breakfast).
    a. *colazione*
    b. *cena*
    c. *pranzo*

22. *È l'* _____ (1:45).
    a. *una a trenta*
    b. *una e quarantacinque*
    c. *una e quindici*

23. *Venga* _____ (tomorrow morning).
    a. *ieri mattina*
    b. *domani mattina*
    c. *domani a mezzogiorno*

24. *In che* _____ (can I) *servirla?*
    a. *può*
    b. *posso*
    c. *possono*

25. *Non* _____ (has) *importanza.*
    a. *avere*
    b. *ha*
    c. *avuto*

ANSWERS

1-b; 2-a; 3-b; 4-c; 5-a; 6-c; 7-a; 8-a; 9-a; 10-c; 11-a;
12-a; 13-b; 14-a; 15-a; 16-b; 17-c; 18-b; 19-b; 20-a;
21-a; 22-b; 23-b; 24-b; 25-b.

SUMMARY OF ITALIAN GRAMMAR
1. ALPHABET

Letter	Name	Letter	Name	Letter	Name
a	a	h	acca	q	qu
b	bi	i	i	r	erre
c	ci	l	elle	s	esse
d	di	m	emme	t	ti
e	e	n	enne	u	u
f	effe	o	o	v	vu
g	gi	p	pi	z	zeta

2. PRONUNCIATION

SIMPLE VOWELS

a	as in *ah* or *father*
e	as in *day, ace*
i	as in *machine, police*
o	as in *no, note*
u	as in *rule*

VOWEL COMBINATIONS

ai	ai in *aisle*
au	ou in *out*
ei	ay-ee
eu	ay-oo
ia	ya in *yard*
ie	ye in *yes*
io	yo in *yoke*
iu	you
oi	oy in *boy*

ua	wah
ue	way
ui	oo-ee
uo	oo-oh

CONSONANTS

h is never pronounced

ll
mm When two consonants occur in the middle of
nn a word, they are both pronounced. Notice the
rr difference between:
ss

caro	dear	*carro*	truck
casa	house	*cassa*	case
pala	shovel	*palla*	ball

SPECIAL ITALIAN SOUNDS

1. *cci, cce* is pronounced like the English *ch* in
   chair:

cacciatore   hunter

2. *ch* before *e* and *i* is pronounced like the English
   k in *key:*

chitarra   guitar

3. *gh* before *e* and *i* is pronounced like the English
   g in *gate:*

ghirlanda   garland

4. *gli.* The closest English approximation is the
   combination *lli* as in *million:*

egli   he   *paglia*   straw

5. *gn* is always pronounced as one letter, somewhat
   like the English *ni* in *onion* or *ny* in *canyon:*

segno   sign   *Spagna*   Spain

6. *sc* before *e* and *i* is pronounced like the English *sh* in *shoe*:

scendere   (to) descend   *sciroppo*   syrup

7. *sc* before *a, o* and *u* is pronounced like the English *sk* in *sky*:

scuola   school   *scarpa*   shoe

3. STRESS

1. Words of two syllables are generally stressed on the first syllable, unless the other one bears an accent mark:

lapis	pencil	*città*	city
penna	pen	*virtù*	virtue
meta	goal	*metà*	half

2. Words of more than two syllables are generally stressed either on the syllable before the last, or on the syllable before that:

ancòra	more	*àncora*	anchor
dolòre	grief	*amòre*	love
scàtola	box	*automòbile*	car

4. USE OF THE DEFINITE ARTICLE

il and *lo* (masc. sing.)   *la* (fem. sing.)
i and *gli* (masc. pl.)   *le* (fem. pl.)

There are instances in which Italian uses a definite article where no article is used in English:

Il tempo è denaro.	Time is money.
La vita è piena di guai.	Life is full of troubles.
I lupi sono feroci.	Wolves are ferocious.
I cani sono fedeli.	Dogs are faithful.
L'oro è un metallo prezioso.	Gold is a precious metal.

Il ferro è duro.	Iron is hard.
Gli affari sono affari.	Business is business.
La necessità non conosce legge.	Necessity knows no law.

Remember that in Italian you generally find the definite article in front of a possessive adjective or pronoun:

Il mio libro è nero, il tuo rosso.	My book is black, yours red.

But with relationship nouns in the singular, no article is used with the possessive adjective:

mio padre	my father
tuo fratello	your brother
nostro zio	our uncle

Only with *loro* (their or your), with *nonno, nonna* (grandfather and grandmother), and with *papà, mamma* (daddy, mamma) is the definite article used with the possesive:

la loro madre	their mother
il vostro nonno	your grandfather

In expressions like the following, Italian uses the definite article:

Tre volte la settimana.	Three times a week.
Due dollari la libbra.	Two dollars a pound.

The definite article is used when talking about parts of the human body.

Il signore ha il naso lungo longo.	The gentleman has a long nose.

The definite article is always used with expressions of time:

Sono le due.	It is two o'clock.

With some geographical expressions:

L'Europa è un continente.	Europe is a continent.
Il Tevere è un fiume.	The Tiber is a river.

5. USE OF THE INDEFINITE ARTICLE

Un, uno, una

Italian uses no indefinite article in cases like the following ones:

Io sono maestro.	I am a teacher.
Che donna!	What a woman!
mezzo quilo	half a kilo
cento uomini	a hundred men

6. THE PLURAL

There is no special plural form for:

1. Nouns with a written accent on the last vowel:

la città	the city
le città	the cities
la virtù	the virtue
le virtù	the virtues

2. Nouns ending in the singular in *i*, and almost all the nouns in *ie:*

il brindisi	the toast
i brindisi	the toasts
la crisi	the crisis
le crisi	the crises
la superficie	the surface
le superficie	the surfaces

3. Nouns ending in a consonant:

il lapis	the pencil
i lapis	the pencils
il gas	the gas
i gas	the gases

7. THE PARTITIVE

1. The partitive is expressed in Italian in several ways:

   a. with the preposition di + a form of the definite article *il, lo, la:*

Io mangio del pane.	I eat some (of the) bread.
Io mangio della carne.	I eat some meat.
Io prendo dello zucchero.	I take some sugar.
Io leggo dei libri.	I read some books.
Io scrivo degli esercizi.	I write some exercises.
Io compro delle sedie.	I buy some chairs.

   b. by using *qualche* (only with singular nouns):

Io scrivo qualche lettera.	I write a few letters.
Io leggo qualche giornale.	I read a few (some) newspapers.

   c. by using *alcuni, alcune,* (only in the plural):

Io ho alcuni amici.	I have a few friends.
Io compongo alcune poesie.	I compose few poems.

   d. by using *un po' di:*

Io prendo un po' di zucchero.	I'll take some sugar.

2. In some cases, especially if the sentence is negative, Italian does not use any partitive at all:

Io non mangio cipolle.	I don't eat onions.

8. ADJECTIVES

1. Many adjectives end in *o* for the masculine:

SINGULAR

un caro amico	a dear friend *(masc.)*

In *a* for the feminine:

una cara amica	a dear friend *(fem.)*

PLURAL

In *i* for the masculine:

cari amici	dear friends *(masc.)*

In *e* for the feminine:

care amiche	dear friends *(fem.)*

2. Some adjectives end in *e* and have the same form in the feminine:

un uomo gentile	a kind man
una donna gentile	a kind woman

In the plural these same adjectives end in *i*, in both the masculine and the feminine:

uomini gentili	kind men
donne gentili	kind women

9. POSITION OF THE ADJECTIVE

A qualifying adjective generally follows the noun if it adds something important to the noun; otherwise it precedes. Some qualifying adjectives, as adjectives of nationality or of color, usually come after the noun:

la musica italiana	Italian music
il libro nero	the black book

Possessive adjectives, demonstrative adjectives, numerals, and indefinite adjectives generally precede the noun:

il mio amico	my friend
questo libro	this book
due penne	two pens
alcuni signori	a few men

10. COMPARISON

Più . . . di or *che*	more . . . than
meno . . . di or *che*	less . . . than
così . . . come	as . . . as
tanto . . . quanto	as much . . . as

After *più* and *meno,* either *di* or *che* can be used, but if the comparison is between two adjectives, or if there is a preposition, only *che* can be used:

Franco è più studioso di (or *che) Carlo.*	Frank is more studious than Charles.
Giacomo è più studioso che intelligente	James is more studious than intelligent.
Ci sono più fanciulli in città che in campagna.	There are more children in the city than in the country.

If the second term of the comparison is expressed by a pronoun, the object form is used:

Egli è più alto di me.	He is taller than I.
Io sono meno ricco di te.	I am less rich than you.
Ella è còsi coraggiosa come lui.	She is as brave as he.

SPECIAL USES OF THE COMPARATIVE

Some expressions with the comparative:

ancora del (dello, della, dei, etc.)	more
un po'più di	a little more
altro, -a, -i, -e	more
Voglio ancora del pane.	I want more bread.
Prendo un po'più di carne.	I take a little more meat.
Compriamo altri libri.	We buy more books.
Non più (quantity)	no more
non più (time)	no longer
Volete di più? No, non vogliamo di più.	Do you want more? No, we want no more.
Ella non canta più.	She sings no longer.
Tanto meglio!	So much the better!
Tanto peggio!	So much the worse!

11. SUPERLATIVE

1. The superlative is formed by dropping the last vowel of the adjective and adding *-issimo, -issima, -issimi, -issime:*

L'esercizio è facilissimo.	The exercise is very easy.

2. by putting in front of the adjectives the words *molto,* or *troppo,* or *assai:*

La poesia è molto bella.	The poem is very beautiful.

12. IRREGULAR COMPARATIVES and SUPERLATIVES

Buono (good):	*migliore, ottimo*
Cattivo (bad):	*peggiore, pessimo*
Grande (great, big):	*maggiore, massimo*
Piccolo (small, little):	*minore, minimo*

Il cameriere è lento.	The waiter is (very) slow.

b. by using a second adjective of almost the same meaning:

La casa è piena zeppa di amici.	The house is full of (loaded with) friends.

c. by using *stra-*, or *arci-*:

Il signore è straricco, (or) *il signore è arciricco.*	The gentleman is loaded with money.

13. DIMINUTIVES and AUGMENTATIVES

1. The endings *-ino*, *-ina*, *-ello*, *-ella*, *-etto*, *-etta*, *-uccio*, *-uccia* imply smallness:

cagnolino	little dog
gattino	kitty

2 The endings *-one*, *-ona*, *-otta* imply largeness:

omone	big man
stupidone	big fool

3. The endings *-ino*, *-uccio* indicate endearment:

tesoruccio	little treasure
caruccia	little darling

4. The endings *-accio*, *-accia*, *-astro*, *-astra*, *-azzo*, *-azza* indicate depreciation:

cagnaccio	ugly dog

14. MASCULINE and FEMININE

Nouns referring to males are masculine; nouns referring to females are feminine:

il padre	the father	*la madre*	the mother
il figlio	the son	*la figlia*	the daughter

l'uomo	the man	*la donna*	the woman
il toro	the bull	*la vacca*	the cow
il gatto	the tomcat	*la gatta*	the female cat

MASCULINE NOUNS

1. Nouns ending in *-o* are usually masculine:

il corpo	the body
il cielo	the sky
il denaro	the money

2. The names of the months and the names of the days (except Sunday) are masculine:

| *il gennaio* | January |
| *il lunedì* | Monday |

3. The names of lakes and many names of mountains are masculine:

| *il Garda* | Lake Garda |
| *gli Appennini* | the Appenines |

FEMININE NOUNS

Nouns ending in *-a* are usually feminine:

la testa	the head
la città	the city
la quantità	the quantity

Nouns ending in *-e*

Nouns ending in *-e* in the singular may be either masculine or feminine:

la madre	the mother
il padre	the father
la legge	the law
il piede	the foot

NOUNS WITH MASCULINE AND FEMININE FORMS

1. Some masculine nouns ending in *-a, -e, -o* form their feminine in *-essa:*

il poeta	the poet	*la poetessa*	the poetess
il conte	the count	*la contessa*	the countess

2. Masculine nouns in *-tore* form their feminine in *-trice:*

l'attore	the actor	*l'attrice*	the actress

15. PLURAL OF NOUNS

1. Nouns ending in *-o*, mostly masculine, form their plural in *-i:*

il lupo	the wolf	*il lupi*	the wolves

SOME EXCEPTIONS:

Nouns ending in *-o* which are, however, feminine:

la mano	the hand	*le mani*	the hands
la radio	the radio	*le radio*	the radios
la dinamo	the dynamo	*le dinamo*	the dynamos

Masculine nouns in *-o* which have two plurals with different meanings for each plural:

il braccio	the arm
i bracci	the arms (of a stream)
le braccia	the arms (of the body)

2. Nouns ending in *-a*, usually feminine, form their plural in *-e:*

la rosa	the rose	*le rose*	the roses

A number of masculine nouns ending in *-a* form their plural in *-i:*

il poeta	the poet	*i poeti*	the poets

3. Nouns ending in *-e,* which can be masculine or feminine, form their plural in *-i:*

il nipote	the nephew or grandson	*i nipoti*	the nephews or grandsons
la nipote	the niece or granddaughter	*le nipoti*	the nieces or granddaughters

SPECIAL CASES

1. Nouns ending in *-ca* or *-ga* insert *h* in the plural:

la barca	the boat	*le barche*	the boats
il monarca	the monarch	*i monarchi*	the monarchs

Exception:

un Belga	a Belgian	*i Belgi*	the Belgians

2. Nouns ending in *-cia* or *-gia* (with unaccented *i*) form their plural in *-ce* or *-ge* if the *c* or *g* are double or preceded by another consonant:

la spiaggia	the sea shore	*le spiagge*	the sea shores
la guancia	the cheek	*le guance*	the cheeks

Nouns ending in *-cia* or *-gia* form their plural in *-cie* or *-gie* if *c* or *g* is preceded by a vowel or if the *i* is accented:

la fiducia	the trust	*le fiducie*	the trusts
le bugia	the lie	*le bugie*	the lies

3. Nouns ending in *-io* (without an accent on the *i*) have a single *i* in the plural:

il figlio	the son	*i figli*	the sons

If the *i* is accented, the plural has *ii:*

lo zio	the uncle	*gli zii*	the uncles

4. Nouns ending in *-co* or *-go* form their plural in *-chi* or *-ghi*, if the accent falls on the syllable before the last:

il fico   the fig   *i fichi*   the figs

Exception:

l'amico   the friend   *gli amici*   the friends

If the accent falls on the second syllables before the last, the plural is in *-ci* or *-gi:*

il medico   the doctor   *i medici*   the doctors

5. Nouns in the singular with the accent on the last vowel do not change in the plural:

la città, le città   the city, the cities

16. THE DAYS OF THE WEEK

The days of the week (except Sunday) are masculine and are not capitalized. The article is unnecessary unless "on Sundays" "on Mondays," etc. is meant.

lunedì	Monday
martedì	Tuesday
mercoledì	Wednesday
giovedì	Thursday
venerdì	Friday
sabato	Saturday
domenica (fem.)	Sunday
Domenica è il primo giorno della settimana.	Sunday is the first day of the week.
Andranno a far loro visita domenica.	They're going to pay them a visit on Sunday.
Domani è sabato.	Tomorrow is Saturday.
La domenica vado in chiesa.	On Sundays I go to church.
Vado a scuola il venerdì.	I go to school on Fridays.

Note: The word "on" is not translated before the days of the week or a date.

il 15 febbraio	on February 15

17. THE NAMES OF THE MONTHS

The names of the months are masculine and are not capitalized. They are usually used without the definite article:

gennaio	January
febbraio	February
marzo	March
aprile	April
maggio	May
giugno	June
luglio	July
agosto	August
settembre	September
ottobre	October
novembre	November
dicembre	December

18. THE NAMES OF THE SEASONS

l' inverno (masc.)	winter
la primavera	spring
l' estate (fem.)	summer
l' autunno (masc.)	fall

The names of the seasons are usually not capitalized. They are preceded by the definite article, but after *di* the article may or may not be used:

L'inverno è una brutta stagione.	Winter is an ugly season.

Fa freddo d' inverno.	It's cold in (the) winter.
Io lavoro durante i mesi d'estate (or dell'estate).	I work during the summer months.

19. NUMBERS

The plural of *mille* (thousand) is *mila; duemila,* two thousand; *seimila,* six thousand.

After *milione* the preposition *di* is used:

un milione di soldati	one million soldiers
tre milioni di dollari	three million dollars

In writing a date, give first the day and then the month:

5 (cinque) agosto	August 5th
10 (dieci) novembre	November 10th

Only for the first of the month is the ordinal numeral used:

il primo novembre	November 1st

20. THE DEMONSTRATIVE

questo, -a,-i, -e	this, these
quello, -a, -i,-e	that, those

The pronoun "this" is *questi:*

Questi è l'uomo che cerchiamo.	This is the man we are looking for.

Besides the forms of *quello* already given, there are also the forms *quel, quei, quegli.* Here is how they are used:

1. If the article *il* is used before the noun, use *quel:*

il libro	the book
quel libro	that book

2. If *i* is used before the noun, use *quei:*

i maestri	the teachers
quei maestri	those teachers

3. If *gli* is used before the noun, use *quegli:*

gli scolari	the students
quegli scolari	those students

The same forms and the same rules apply to *bel, bei, begli,* from *bello, -a, -i, -e,* beautiful.

21. POSSESSIVE ADJECTIVES

Always use the article in front of a possessive adjective:

il mio denaro	my money
la tua sedia	your chair
la vostra borsa	your pocketbook

except for members of the family in the singular:

mia madre	my mother

The possessive adjective agrees with the thing possessed and not with the possessor:

la sua chiave	(his, her) key

Suo may mean *his* or *her* or, with the polite form, *your*. If confusion should arise by using *suo*, use *di lui, di lei,* etc.

22. INDEFINITE ADJECTIVES

1. *qualche* (used only   some
   in *sing.*)
   alcuni (used only   some
   in the *pl.*)

qualche lettera	some letters
alcuni dollari	some dollars

Note: *Alcuni* can be also used as a pronoun:
alcuni . . . altri (some . . . others).

2. *qualunque, qualsiasi*   any
   (has no *pl.*)

Qualunque mese	any month
qualsiasi ragazzo	any boy

3. *ogni* (has no *pl.*)   every or each
ciascun, ciascuno,   each or every
   ciascuna (no *pl.*)

Ogni ragazzo parla.	Every boy talks.
Ogni ragazza parla.	Every girl talks.
Diciamo una parola a ciascun signore.	Let's say a word to each gentlemen.
Raccontate tutto a ciascuna signora.	Tell everything to each (or every) lady.

4. *altro (l'altro), altra,*   other or more
   altri, altre

Mandiamo gli altri libri?	Do we send the other books?
Vuole altro denaro?	Do you want more money?

5. *nessuno, nessun,*   no, no one
   nessuna

Nessuno zio ha scritto.	No uncle wrote.
Nessun soldato ha paura.	No soldier is afraid.
Nessuna sedia è buona.	No chair is good.

23. INDEFINITE PRONOUNS

1. *alcuni*	some
alcuni . . . altri	some . . . some

alcuni dei suoi discorsi	some of his speeches
Di questi libri a alcuni sono buoni, altri cattivi.	Of these books some are good, some bad.

2. *qualcuno, qualcheduno* — someone, somebody (no *fem.*, no *pl.*)

Qualcuno è venuto.	Somebody came.
Qualcheduno ci chiama	Somebody is calling us.

3. *chiunque, chicchessia* — anybody, any one (no *fem.*, no *pl.*)

Chiunque dice così	Anybody says so.

4. *ognuno* (only *sing.*), *tutti* (only *pl.*) } everybody, everyone

ciascuno (only *sing.*), *tutto* — each or each one, everything

Ognuno corre.	Everybody runs.
Tutti corrono.	Everybody runs (all run).

5. *l'altro, l'altra, gli altri, le altre, altro* — the other, the others. *(in interrogative or negative sentences)* else, anything else

un altro — another one

Egli dice una cosa, ma l'altro non è d'accordo.	He says one thing, but the other one does not agree.
Volete altro?	Do you want something else?
Non vogliamo altro.	We do not want anything else.

6. *niente, nulla* — nothing

nessuno (no *fem.*, no *pl.*) — nobody, no one

Niente (nulla) lo consola	Nothing consoles him.
Nessuno conosce questa regola.	Nobody knows this rule.

24. INTERROGATIVE PRONOUNS and ADJECTIVES

1. The interrogative pronoun *chi* refers to persons, and corresponds to *who* or *whom or which*, as illustrated by the three examples following:

Chi vi scrive?	Who writes to you?
Chi vediamo?	Whom do we see?
Chi di noi ha parlato?	Which of us has talked?

2. *che* or *che cosa* translates *what*:

Che facciamo?	What are we doing?
Che cosa leggete?	What are you reading?

3. The two interrogative adjectives *quale* and *che* mean *which, what*:

Quale dei due giornali compra lei?	Which of the two newspapers do you buy?
Che colore desiderate?	What color do you wish?

25. RELATIVE PRONOUNS

chi	he who, him who
che	who, whom, that, which
cui	(used with prepositions)
di cui	of whom, of which
in cui	in which

Chi studia impara.	He who studies, learns.
l'uomo che ho visto	the man whom I saw
la donna di cui parlo	the woman of whom I speak

1. *che:* (undeclinable) For masculine, feminine, singular, plural; for persons, animals, things. Do not use this pronoun if there is a preposition.

2. *il quale, la quale, i quali, le quali:* For persons, animals, things, with the same English meanings as *che;* can be used with or without prepositions.

3. *cui:* (undeclinable) Masculine, feminine, singular, plural; for persons, animals, things; is always used with a preposition.

26. PERSONAL PRONOUNS

Pronouns have different forms depending on whether they are:

1. the subject of a verb
2. the direct object of a verb
3. the indirect object of a verb
4. used after a preposition
5. used with reflexive verbs

1. The subject pronouns are:

	SINGULAR
io	I
tu	you
egli	he
ella	she
lei	you
esso	he, it
essa	she, it

PLURAL

noi	we
voi	you
essi	they *(masc.)*
esse	they *(fem.)*
loro	you, they

It is not necessary to use subject pronouns as the verb ending indicates who is speaking or being spoken about.

2. The direct object pronouns are:

mi	me
ti	you
lo	him, it
la	her, it, you
ci	us
vi	you
li	them, you
le	them, you
Ci vede.	He sees us.
Lo scrive.	He writes it.

3. The indirect object pronouns are:

mi	to me
ti	to you
gli	to him
le	to her, to you
ci	to us
vi	to you
loro	to them, to you
Egli mi scrive una lettera.	He is writing me a letter.
Io ti regalo una bambola.	I am giving you a doll.
Noi parliamo loro.	We speak to them.

4. The pronouns used after a preposition are:

me	me
te	you

lui	him
lei	her, you
noi	us
voi	you
loro	them, you

Io verrò con te.	I shall come with you.
Egli parla sempre di lei.	He always speaks about her.

5. The reflexive pronouns are:

mi	myself
ti	yourself
si	himself, herself, itself, yourself
ci	ourselves
vi	yourselves
si	themselves, yourselves

Io mi lavo.	I wash myself.
Noi ci diamo la mano.	We shake hands.
Essi si alzano.	They get up.

27. POSITION OF PRONOUNS

1. Pronouns are written as separate words, except with the imperative, infinitive, and gerund, where they follow the verbal form and are written as one word with it:

Ditelo.	Say it.
Fatemi un favore.	Do me a favor.
facendovi . . .	doing it . . .

chiamandolo	calling him
scriverle una lettera	to write her a letter
dopo avermi chiamato	after having called me

2. In the imperative, when the polite form is used, the pronouns are never attached to the verb:

Mi faccia un favore.	Do me a favor.

3. Some verbs of one syllable in the imperative double the initial consonant of the pronoun:

Dimmi una cosa.	Tell me one thing.
Facci una cortesia.	Do us a favor.

4. In the compound infinitive the pronoun is generally attached to the auxiliary:

Credo di averti dato tutto.	I think I gave you everything.

The simple infinitive drops the final *e* before the pronoun:

leggere un articolo	to read an article
leggerti un articolo	to read you an article

5. When two object pronouns are used with the same verb, the indirect precedes the direct:

Io te lo voglio dire.	I want to tell it to you.

Observe the following changes in the pronouns which occur in this case:

The *i* in *mi, ti, ci, vi, si* changes to *e* before *lo, la, le, li, ne,* while *gli* takes an additional *e* and is written as one word with the following pronoun. *Le* also becomes *glie* before *lo, la, li, le, ne*:

Ce lo dà.	He gives it to us.
Glielo mando a casa.	I send it home to him (to her, to you).
Glielo dicono.	They tell it to him (to her, to you).

28. NE

1. Used as a pronoun meaning *of him, of her, of them, of it:*

Parla lei del mio amico?	Are you talking of my friend?
Sì, ne parlo.	Yes, I am talking of him.
Parliamo noi di questa cosa?	Are we talking of this thing?
Sì, ne parliamo.	Yes, we are talking of it.

2. Used as a partitive meaning *some* or *any:*

Mangi la signorina del pesce?	Does the young lady eat some fish?
Sì, ne mangia.	Yes, she does (eat some).

3. Used as an adverb of place, meaning *from* or *out of:*

Gli studenti escono dalla classe?	Are the students coming out from the class?
Sì, ne escono.	Yes, they are (coming out).

29. SI

1. *Si* can be used as a reflexive pronoun:

Egli si lava.	He washes himself.
Essi si lavano.	They wash themselves.

2. *Si* is used as an impersonal pronoun:

Non sempre si riflette su quel che si dice.	Not always does one ponder over what one says.
Qui si mangia bene.	Here one eats well.

3. *Si* is sometimes used to translate the English passive:

Come si manda questa lettera?	How is this letter sent?

30. ADVERBS

1. Many adverbs end in *-mente:*

caramente	dearly
dolcemente	sweetly

These adverbs are easily formed; take the feminine singular form of the adjective and add *-mente.* For instance, "dear" = Italian *caro, cara, cari, care* (an adjective of the so-called first group); the feminine singular is *cara,* and so the adverb will be *caramente.* "Sweet" is *dolce, dolci* (an adjective of the second group; these adjectives show no difference between the masculine and feminine); the feminine singular is *dolce,* and so the adverb will be *dolcemente.*

2. Adjectives ending in *-le* or *-re,* if the *l* or *r* is preceded by a vowel, drop the final *e* before *-mente;* thus the adverb corresponding to *facile* is *facilmente* (easily); *celere* (fast) becomes *celermente* (fast, *adv.*). The adverbs corresponding to *buono* (good) and *cattivo* (bad) are *bene* and *male.*

3. Adverbs may have a comparative and superlative form:
Caramente, più caramente, molto caramente, or *carissimamente.*

Observe these irregular comparative and superlative forms of adverbs:

meglio	better
peggio	worse
maggiormente	more greatly
massimamente	very greatly
minimamente	in the least
ottimamente	very well
pessimamente	very bad

31. PREPOSITIONS

a. The most common prepositions in Italian are:

1. *di*	of
2. *a*	at, to
3. *da*	from
4. *in*	in
5. *con*	with
6. *su, sopra*	above
7. *per*	through, by means of, on
8. *tra, fra*	between, among

b. When used in connection with the definite article, they are often contracted. Here are the most common of these combinations:

di + il = del	*a + il = al*
di + lo = dello	*a + lo = allo*
di + la = della	*a + la = alla*
di + l' = dell'	*a + l' = all'*
di + i = dei	*a + gli = agli*
di + gli = degli	*a + le = alle*
di + le = delle	

con + il = col	*sul + il = sul*
con + i = coi	*su + la = sulla*
	su + lo = sullo
	su + gli = sugli
	su + i = sui

Io ho del denaro.	I have some money.
il cavallo dello zio	the uncle's horse
Io regalo un dollaro al ragazzo.	I give a dollar to the boy.
Il professore risponde agli studenti.	The professor answers the students.

32. NEGATION

1. *Non* (not) comes before the verb:

Io non vedo.	I don't see.
Egli non parla.	He isn't speaking.

2. nothing, never, no one:

Non vedo nulla.	I see nothing.
Non vado mai.	I never go.
Non viene nessuno. }	No one comes.
Nessuno viene.	

(If the negative pronoun begins the sentence, *non* is not used . . .)

33. QUESTION WORDS

1.	*Che?*	What?
	Che cosa?	What?
2.	*Perchè?*	Why?
3.	*Come?*	How?
4.	*Quanto?*	How much?
5.	*Quando?*	When?
6.	*Dove?*	Where?
7.	*Quale?*	Which?

34. THE TENSES OF THE VERB

A. Italian verbs are divided into three classes (conjugations) according to their infinitives:

Class I —*parlare, amare*
Class II —*scrivere, temere*
Class III—*partire, sentire*

1. The Present:

First Conj. (I)	Second Conj. (II)	Third Conj. (III)
-o	*-o*	*-o*
-i	*-i*	*-i*
-a	*-e*	*-e*
-iamo	*-iamo*	*-iamo*
-ate	*-ete*	*-ite*
-ano	*-ono*	*-ono*

The present tense can be translated in several ways:

Io parlo italiano
{ I speak Italian.
I am speaking Italian.
I do speak Italian.

2. The Imperfect:

I.	II.	III.
-avo	*-evo*	*-ivo*
-avi	*-evi*	*-ivi*
-ava	*-eva*	*-iva*
-avamo	*-evamo*	*-ivamo*
-avate	*-evate*	*-ivate*
-avano	*-evano*	*-ivano*

The Imperfect is used:

a. To indicate continued or customary action in the past:

| *Quando ero a Roma, andavo sempre a visitare i musei.* | When I was in Rome, I was always visiting the museums. |
| *Lo incontravo ogni giorno.* | I used to meet him every day. |

b. To indicate what was happening when something else happened:

| *Egli scriveva quando ella entrò.* | He was writing when she entered. |

3. The Future:

The future of regular verbs is formed by adding to the infinitive (after the final *e* is dropped) the endings *-ò; -ai; -à; -emo; -ete; -anno.* For the first conjugation, the *a* of the infinitive changes to *e*.

The future generally expresses action which will take place in the future.

Lo comprerò.	I'll buy it.
Andrò domani.	I'll go tomorrow.

Sometimes it expresses probability or conjecture:

Che ora sarà?	What time can it be? What time do you think it must be?
Sarà l'una.	It must be almost one.
Starà mangiando ora.	He's probably eating now.

4. *Passato remoto* (preterit, past definite):

This tense indicates an action which happened in a period of time completely finished now:

Romolo fondò Roma.	Romulus founded Rome.
Dante nacque nel 1265.	Dante was born in 1265.
Garibaldi combattè per l'unità d'Italia.	Garibaldi fought for the unity of Italy.

5. *Passato prossimo* (compound past):

The *passato prossimo* is formed by adding the past participle to the present indicative of *avere* or *essere*. It is used to indicate a past action and corresponds to the English preterit or perfect:

Io ho finito il mio lavoro.	I finished my work. (I have finished my work.)
L'hai visto?	Have you seen him?
Sono arrivati.	They arrived.

6. The pluperfect tense is formed by adding the past participle to the imperfect of *avere* or *essere*. It translates the English past perfect:

Egli l'aveva fatto.	He had done it.

7. The *trapassato remoto* is formed by adding the past participle to the past definite of *avere* or *essere*. It is used to indicate an event that had happened just before another event:

Quando usci ebbe finito.	When he had finished, he went out.

8. The future perfect tense is formed by adding the past participle to the future of *avere* or *essere*. It translates to the English future perfect:

Egli avrà finito presto.	He will soon have finished.

Sometimes it indicates probability:

Quando egli avrà finito, andrà a casa.	When he has finished, he will go home.
Egli sara stato ammalato.	He probably was sick.

B. Complete conjugation of a sample verb from each class:

Amare (First Conjugation): to love, like

INDICATIVE

PRESENT	IMPERFECT
io amo	*io amavo*
tu ami	*tu amavi*
egli ama	*egli amava*
noi amiamo	*noi amavamo*
voi amate	*voi amavate*
essi amano	*essi amavano*

FUTURE

io amerò
tu amerai
egli amerà
noi ameremo
voi amerete
essi ameranno

PRETERIT

io amai
tu amasti
egli amò
noi amammo
voi amaste
essi amarono

PRETERIT PERFECT

io ebbi amato
tu avesti amato
egli ebbe amato
noi avemmo amato
voi aveste amato
essi ebbero amato

PRESENT PERFECT

io hoi amato
tu hai amato
egli ha amato
noi abbiamo amato
voi avete amato
essi hanno amato

PLUPERFECT

io avevo amato
tu avevi amato
egli aveva amato
noi avevamo amato
voi avevate amato
essi avevano amato

FUTURE PERFECT

io avrò amato
tu avrai amato
egli avrà amato
noi avremo amato
voi avrete amato
essi avranno amato

SUBJUNCTIVE

PRESENT

io ami
tu ami
egli ami
noi amiamo
voi amiate
essi amino

PERFECT

io abbia amato
tu abbia amato

IMPERFECT

io amassi
tu amassi
egli amasse
noi amassimo
voi amaste
essi amassero

PLUPERFECT

io avessi amato
tu avessi amato

egli abbia amato   egli avesse amato
noi abbiamo amato   noi avessimo amato
voi abbiate amato   voi aveste amato
essi abbiano amato   essi avessero amato

IMPERATIVE

PRESENT

ama (tu)
ami (lei)
amiamo (noi)
amate (voi)
amino (loro)

CONDITIONAL

PRESENT	PERFECT
io amerei	io avrei amato
tu ameresti	tu avresti amato
egli amerebbe	egli avrebbe amato
noi ameremmo	noi avremmo amato
voi amereste	voi avreste amato
essi amerebbero	essi avrebbero amato

INFINITIVES

PRESENT	PERFECT
amare	avere amato

PARTICIPLES

PRESENT	PERFECT
amante	amato

GERUNDS

PRESENT	PERFECT
amando	avendo amato

Temere (Second Conjugation): to fear

INDICATIVE

PRESENT

io temo
tu temi
egli teme
noi temiamo
voi temete
essi temono

IMPERFECT

io temevo
tu temevi
egli temeva
noi temevamo
voi temevate
essi temevano

FUTURE

io temerò
tu temerai
egli temerà
noi temeremo
voi temerete
essi temeranno

PRESENT PERFECT

io ho temuto
tu hai temuto
egli ha temuto
noi abbiamo temuto
voi avete temuto
essi hanno temuto

PRETERIT

io temei (or -*etti*)
tu temesti
egli temè (or -*ette*)
noi tememmo
voi temeste
essi temerono (or
  -*ettero*)

PLUPERFECT

io avevo temuto
tu avevi temuto
egli aveva temuto
noi avevamo temuto
voi avevate temuto
essi avevano temuto

PRETERIT PERFECT

io ebbi temuto
tu avesti temuto
egli ebbe temuto
noi avemmo temuto
voi aveste temuto
essi ebbero temuto

FUTURE PERFECT

io avrò temuto
tu avrai temuto
egli avrà temuto
noi avremo temuto
voi avrete temuto
essi avranno temuto

SUBJUNCTIVE

PRESENT	IMPERFECT
io tema	*io temessi*
tu tema	*tu temessi*
egli tema	*egli temesse*
noi temiamo	*noi temessimo*
voi temiate	*voi temeste*
essi temano	*essi temessero*

PERFECT	PLUPERFECT
io abbia temuto	*io avessi temuto*
tu abbia temuto	*tu avessi temuto*
egli abbia temuto	*egli avesse temuto*
noi abbiamo temuto	*noi avessimo temuto*
voi abbiate temuto	*voi aveste temuto*
essi abbiano temuto	*essi avessero temuto*

IMPERATIVE

PRESENT

temi (tu)
tema (lei)
temiamo (noi)
temete (voi)
temano (loro)

CONDITIONAL

PRESENT	PERFECT
io temerei	*io avrei temuto*
tu temeresti	*tu avresti temuto*
egli temerebbe	*egli avrebbe temuto*
noi temeremmo	*noi avremmo temuto*
voi temereste	*voi avreste temuto*
essi temerebbero	*essi avrebbero temuto*

INFINITIVES

PRESENT	PERFECT
temere	*aver temuto*

PARTICIPLES

PRESENT	PERFECT
temente	*temuto*

GERUNDS

PRESENT	PERFECT
temendo	*avendo temuto*

Sentire (Third Conjugation):

INDICATIVE

PRESENT	IMPERFECT
io sento	*io sentivo*
tu senti	*tu sentivi*
egli sente	*egli sentiva*
noi sentiamo	*noi sentivamo*
voi sentite	*voi sentivate*
essi sentono	*essi sentivano*

FUTURE	PRESENT PERFECT
io sentirò	*io ho sentito*
tu sentirai	*tu hai sentito*
egli sentirà	*egli ha sentito*
noi sentiremo	*noi avevamo sentito*
voi sentirete	*voi avete sentito*
essi sentiranno	*essi hanno sentito*

PRETERIT	PLUPERFECT
io sentii	*io avevo sentito*
tu sentisti	*tu avevi sentito*
egli sentì	*egli aveva sentito*

noi sentimmo
voi sentiste
essi sentirono

noi avevamo sentito
voi avevate sentito
essi avevano sentito

PRETERIT PERFECT

io ebbi sentito
tu avesti sentito
egli ebbe sentito
noi avemmo sentito
voi aveste sentito
essi ebbero sentito

FUTURE PERFECT

io avrò sentito
tu avrai sentito
egli avrà sentito
noi avremo sentito
voi avrete sentito
essi avranno sentito

SUBJUNCTIVE

PRESENT

io senta
tu senta
egli senta
noi sentiamo
voi sentiate
essi sentano

IMPERFECT

io sentissi
tu sentissi
egli sentisse
noi sentissimo
voi sentiste
essi sentissero

PERFECT

io abbia sentito
tu abbia sentito
egli abbia sentito
noi abbiamo sentito
voi abbiate sentito
essi abbiano sentito

PLUPERFECT

io avessi sentito
tu avessi sentito
egli avesse sentito
noi avessimo sentito
voi aveste sentito
essi avessero sentito

IMPERATIVE

PRESENT

(first person: missing)

senti

senta
sentiamo
sentite
sentano

CONDITIONAL

PRESENT	PERFECT
io sentirei	*io avrei sentito*
tu sentiresti	*tu avresti sentito*
egli sentirebbe	*egli avrebbe sentito*
noi sentiremmo	*noi avremmo sentito*
voi sentireste	*voi avreste sentito*
essi sentirebbero	*essi avrebbero sentito*

INFINITIVES

PRESENT	PERFECT
sentire	*aver sentito*

PARTICIPLES

PRESENT	PERFECT
sentente	*sentito*

GERUNDS

PRESENT	PERFECT
sentendo	*avendo sentito*

35. THE PAST PARTICIPLE

1. The past participle ends in:

-ato, (-ata, -ati, -ate) (for the First Conjugation)	*parl - ato*
-uto (for the Second Conjugation)	*bev - uto*

-ito (for the Third   *part -ito*
    Conjugation)

2. The past participle used with *essere* agrees with
the subject of the verb:

è andato   he left
sono andate   they *(fem.)* left

3. The past participle used with *avere* generally
agrees with the preceding direct object:

i libri che ella ha comprati
the books that she bought

i libri che egli ha comprati
the books that he bought

36. USE OF THE AUXILIARIES

The most common intransitive verbs which are conju-
gated with the verb *essere* in the compound tenses are
the following:

*andare, arrivare, scendere, entrare, salire, morire,
nascere, partire, restare, ritornare, uscire, cadere,
venire, rivenire.*

   Io sono venuto.   I have come.
   Egli è arrivato.   He has arrived.
   Noi siamo partiti.   We have left.

Reflexive verbs form their past tenses with *essere*. If
there is a direct object, generally the past participle
agrees with it, and not with the subject:

   La signorina si è rotto il   The young lady broke
     braccio.   her arm.

The past tenses of passive constructions are formed
with *essere:*

   Il ragazzo è amato.   The boy is loved.
   La ragazza è stata   The girl has been loved.
     amata.

I ragazzi furono amati.	The boys were loved.
Le ragazze saranno amate.	The girls will be loved.

Sometimes the verb *venire* is used instead of *essere* in a passive construction:

La poesia è letta dal maestro.	The poem is read by the teacher.
La poesia viene letta dal maestro.	The poem is read by the teacher.

THE PROGRESSIVE PRESENT

Io fumo means "I smoke" or "I am smoking," but there is also a special way of translating "I am smoking": *Io sto fumando.* In other words, Italian uses the verb *stare* with the present gerund of the main verb:

Noi stiamo leggendo.	We are reading.
Egli stava scrivendo.	He was writing.

This form is generally used only in the simple tenses.

37. SUBJUNCTIVE

A. Formation:

1. The Present Tense

   a. First Conjugation: By dropping the *-are* from the infinitive, and adding *-i, -i, -i, -iamo, -iate, -ino*.

Penso che egli parli troppo.	I think (that) he speaks too much.

   b. Second and Third Conjugation: By dropping the *-ere* and *-ire*, and adding *-a, -a, -a, -iamo, -iate, -iano*.

Sebbene lei scriva in fretta, non fa errori.	Although you write fast, you make no mistakes.

2. The Imperfect Tense
   a. First Conjugation: By dropping the *-are,* and adding *-assi, -assi, -asse, -assimo, -aste, -assero.*

Credevo che il ragazzo lavorasse molto.	I thought (that) the boy was working hard.

   b. Second Conjugation: By dropping the *-ere,* and adding *-essi, -essi, -esse, -essimo, -este, -essero.*

Prima che le signorina scrivesse la lettera, il padre la chiamò.	Before the girl could write the letter, her father called her.

   c. Third Conjugation: By dropping the *-ire,* and adding *-issi, -issi, -isse, -issimo, -iste, -issero.*

Ero del parere che il mio amico si sentisse male.	I was under the impression that my friend did not feel well.

3. The Compound Tenses (Perfect and Pluperfect)
   They are formed with the present and imperfect of the subjunctive of "to have" and "to be," and the past participle.

Credo che gli studenti abbiano finito la lezione.	I think (that) the students have finished the lesson.
Era possibile che i mei amici fossero già arrivati in città.	It was possible that my friends had already arrived in town.

B. Uses of the Subjunctive:

The subjunctive mood expresses doubt, uncertainty, hope, fear, desire, supposition, possibility, probability, granting, etc. For this reason, it is mostly found in clauses dependent upon another verb.

1. In a few cases the subjunctive is used alone. The most common ones are:

   a. In exhortations:

Facciamo cosi.	Let us do so.
Pensiamo come fare queste cose.	Let us think how to do these things.

   b. To express a wish or desire:

Siate felici!	May you be happy!

2. The subjunctive is used in dependent clauses in the following ways:

   a. After verbs expressing hope, wish, desire, command, doubt:

Voglio che tu ci vada.	I want you to go there.

   b. After verbs expressing an opinion (*penso, credo*):

Penso che sia vero.	I think it is true.

   c. After expressions made with a form of *essere* and an adjective or an adverb (*è necessario, è facile, è possibile*), or some impersonal expressions like *bisogna, importa,* etc.:

È necessario che io parta subito.	It is necessary that I leave immediately.
È impossibile che noi veniamo questa sera.	It is impossible for us to come this evening.

   d. After some conjunctions—*sebbene, quantunque, per quanto, benchè, affinchè, prima che* (subjunctive to express a possibility; indicative to express a fact):

Sebbene non sia guarito, devo uscire.	Although I am not well yet, I must go out.

| *Quantunque te l'abbia già detto, ricordati di andare alla Posta.* | Although I told you already, remember to go to the Post Office. |

38. THE CONDITIONAL

The conditional is formed:

1. In the present tense:

   a. First and Second Conjugations: By dropping the *-are* or *-ere*, and adding *-erei, -ereste, -erebbe, -eremmo, -ereste, -erebbero.*

| *a signora parlerebbe molto, se potesse.* | The lady would speak a lot if she could. |

   b. Third Conjugation: By dropping the *-ire*, and adding *-irei, -iresti, -irebbe, -iremmo, -ireste, -irebbero.*

| *Il signore si sentirebbe bene, se prendesse le pillole.* | The gentleman would feel well if he took the pills. |

2. In the past tense:

   By using the present of the conditional of "to have" or "to be" and the past participle.

| *Mio cugino non avrebbe investito il suo denaro in questo, se l'avesse saputo primo.* | My cousin would not have invested his money in this, if he had known it before. |

39. THE "IF" CLAUSES

An "if" clause can express:

1. *reality.* In this case the indicative is used:

Se oggi piove, non uscirò.	If it rains to-day, I won't go out.

2. *possibility.* The imperfect subjunctive and the conditional present are used to express possibility in the present:

Se tu leggessi, impareresti.	If you read, you would learn. (The idea is that it is possible that you may read and so you may learn.)

The pluperfect subjunctive and the past conditional are used to express a possibility in the past:

Se tu avessi letto, avresti imparato.	If you had read, you would have learned. (The idea is that you might have read and so might have learned.)

3. *impossibility* or *unreality.* Use the same construction as in number 2; the only difference is that we know that the condition cannot be fulfilled.

Se l'uomo vivesse mille anni, imparerebbe molte cose.	If man lived 1000 years, he would learn many things. (But it's a fact that man doesn't live 1000 years, and so doesn't learn many things.)
Se io avessi studiato quando ero giovane, avrei fatto un gran	If I had studied when I was young, I would have given great

piacere ai miei genitori.

pleasure to my parents. (But it's a fact that I did not study, and so I did not bring great pleasure to my parents.)

40. IMPERATIVE

The forms of the imperative are normally taken from the present indicative:

leggi	read
leggiamo	let us read
leggete	read

For the First Conjugation, however, note:

canta	sing

The polite forms of the imperative are taken from the present subjunctive:

canti	sing
cantino	sing
legga	read
leggano	read

41. "TO BE" AND "TO HAVE"

Essere and *avere*, "to be" and "to have," are very irregular. For your convenience here are their conjugations.

ESSERE:

INDICATIVE

PRESENT

io sono	*noi siamo*
tu sei	*voi siete*
egli è	*essi sono*

IMPERFECT

io ero	noi eravamo
tu eri	voi eravate
egli era	essi erano

FUTURE

io sarò	noi saremo
tu sarai	voi sarete
egli sarà	essi saranno

PRESENT PERFECT

io sono stato	noi siamo stati
tu sei stato	voi siete stati
egli è stato	essi sono stati

PRETERIT

io fui	noi fummo
tu fosti	voi foste
egli fu	essi furono

PLUPERFECT

io ero stato	noi eravamo stati
tu eri stato	voi eravate stati
egli era stato	essi erano stati

PRETERIT PERFECT

io fui stato	noi fummo stati
tu fosti stato	voi foste stati
egli fu stato	essi furono stati

FUTURE PERFECT

io sarò stato	*noi saremo stati*
tu sarai stato	*voi sarete stati*
egli sarà stato	*essi saranno stati*

SUBJUNCTIVE

PRESENT

io sia	*noi siamo*
tu sia	*voi siate*
egli sia	*essi siano*

IMPERFECT

io fossi	*noi fossimo*
tu fossi	*voi foste*
egli fosse	*essi fossero*

PERFECT

io sia stato	*noi siamo stati*
tu sia stato	*voi siate stati*
egli sia stato	*essi siano stati*

PLUPERFECT

io fossi stato	*noi fossimo stati*
tu fossi stato	*voi foste stati*
egli fosse stato	*essi fossero stati*

IMPERATIVE

PRESENT

	(noi) siamo
(tu) sii	(voi) siate
(lei) sia	(loro) siano

CONDITIONAL

PRESENT

io sarei	noi saremmo
tu saresti	voi sareste
egli sarebbe	essi sarebbero

PERFECT

io sarei stato	noi saremmo stati
tu saresti stato	voi sareste stati
egli sarebbe stato	essi sarebbero stati

INFINITIVE

PRESENT	PERFECT
essere	essere stato

PARTICIPLE

PERFECT

stato

GERUND

PRESENT	PERFECT
essendo	*essendo stato*

AVERE:

INDICATIVE

PRESENT

io ho	*noi abbiamo*
tu hai	*voi avete*
egli ha	*essi hanno*

IMPERFECT

io avevo	*noi avevamo*
tu avevi	*voi avevate*
egli aveva	*essi avevano*

FUTURE

io avrò	*noi avremo*
tu avrai	*voi avrete*
egli avrà	*essi avranno*

PRESENT PERFECT

io ho avuto	*noi abbiamo avuto*
tu hai avuto	*voi avete avuto*
egli ha avuto	*essi hanno avuto*

PRETERIT

io ebbi	noi avemmo
tu avesti	voi aveste
egli ebbe	essi ebbero

PLUPERFECT

io avevo avuto	noi avevamo avuto
tu avevi avuto	voi avevate avuto
egli aveva avuto	essi avevano avuto

PRETERIT PERFECT

io ebbi avuto	noi avemmo avuto
tu avesti avuto	voi aveste avuto
egli ebbe avuto	essi ebbero avuto

FUTURE PERFECT

io avrò avuto	noi avremo avuto
tu avrai avuto	voi avrete avuto
egli avrà avuto	essi avranno avuto

SUBJUNCTIVE

PRESENT

io abbia	noi abbiamo
tu abbia	vi abbiate
egli abbia	essi abbiano

IMPERFECT

io avessi	noi avessimo
tu avessi	voi aveste

egli avesse   *essi avessero*

PERFECT

io abbia avuto   *noi abbiamo avuto*
tu abbia avuto   *voi abbiate avuto*
egli abbia avuto   *essi abbiano avuto*

PLUPERFECT

io avessi avuto   *noi avessimo avuto*
tu avessi avuto   *voi aveste avuto*
egli avesse avuto   *essi avessero avuto*

IMPERATIVE

PRESENT

                                (noi) abbiamo
(tu) abbi   *(voi) abbiate*

CONDITIONAL

PRESENT

io avrei   *noi avremmo*
tu avresti   *voi avreste*
egli avrebbe   *essi avrebbero*

PERFECT

io avrei avuto   *noi avremmo avuto*

tu avresti avuto	*voi avreste avuto*
egli avrebbe avuto	*essi avrebbero avuto*

INFINITIVE

PRESENT	PERFECT
avere	*avere avuto*

PARTICIPLES

PRESENT	PERFECT
avente	*avuto*

GERUND

PRESENT	PERFECT
avendo	*avendo avuto*

42. SOME IRREGULAR VERBS

(Only irregular tenses are indicated. Other tenses follow the regular pattern of the conjugation as shown in section 34.)

Andare = to go
Ind. pres.: *vado, vai, va, andiamo, andate, vanno.*
Future: *andrò, andrai, andrà, andremo, andrete, andranno.*
Subj. pres.: *vada, vada, vada, andiamo, andiate, vadano.*
Imperative: *va', vada, andiamo, andate, vadano.*
Cond. pres.: *andrei, andresti, andrebbe, andremmo, etc.*

Bere = to drink

Ind. pres.: *bevo, bevi, beve, beviamo, bevete, bevono.*

Imperfect: *bevevo, bevevi, etc.*

Preterit: *bevvi, bevesti, bevve, bevemmo, beveste, bevvero.*

Future: *berrò, berrai, berrà, berremo, berrete, berrano.*

Subj. imp.: *bevessi, etc.*

Cond. pres.: *berrei, berresti, berrebbe, etc.*

Past part.: *bevuto.*

Cadere = to fall

Future: *cadrò, cadrai, cadrà, cadremo, cadrete, cadranno.*

Preterit: *caddi, cadesti, cadde, cademmo, cadeste, caddero.*

Cond. pres.: *cadrei, cadresti, cadrebbe, etc.*

Chiedere = to ask

Preterit: *chiesi, chiedesti, chiese, chiedemmo, chiedeste, chiesero.*

Past part.: *chiesto*

Chiudere = to shut

Preterit: *chiusi, chiudesti, chiuse, chiudemmo, chiudeste, chiusero.*

Past part.: *chiuso.*

Conoscere = to know

Preterit: *conobbi, conoscesti, conobbe, conoscemmo, conosceste, conobbero.*

Past part.: *conosciuto.*

Cuocere = to cook

Ind. pres.: *cuocio, cuoci, cuoce, cociamo, cocete, cuociono.*

Preterit: *cossi, cocesti, cosse, cocemmo, coceste, cossero.*
Subj. pres.: *cuocia* or *cocia, etc.*
Imperative: *cuoci, cuocia, etc.*
Past part.: *cotto.*

Dare = to give
Ind. pres.: *do, dai, dà, diamo, date, danno.*
Preterit: *diedi* or *detti, desti, diede* or *dette, demmo, deste, dettero* or *diedero.*
Subj. pres.: *dia, dia, dia, diamo, diate, diano.*
Subj. imper.: *dessi, dessi, desse, dessimo, deste, dessero.*
Imperative: *da', dia, diamo, date, diano.*
Past part.: *dato.*

Dire = to say
Ind. pres.: *dico, dici, dice, diciamo, dite, dicono.*
Imperfect: *dicevo, dicevi, etc.*
Preterit: *dissi, dicesti, disse, dicemmo, diceste, dissero.*
Subj. pres.: *dica, dica, dica, diciamo, diciate, dicano.*
Subj. imper.: *dicessi, dicessi, dicesse, dicessimo, diceste, dicerssero.*
Imperative: *di, dica, diciamo, dite, dicano.*
Past part.: *detto.*

Dolere = to suffer, to ache
Ind. pres.: *dolgo, duoli, duole, doliamo, dolete, dolgono.*
Preterit: *dolsi, dolesti, dolse, dolemmo, doleste, dolsero.*
Future: *dorrò, dorrai, dorrà, dorremo, dorrete, dorranno.*

Subj. pres.: *dolga, etc., doliamo, doliate, dolgano.*
Cond. pres.: *dorrei, dorresti, dorrebbe, etc.*

Dovere = to owe, to be obliged
Ind. pres.: *devo* or *debbo, devi, deve, dobbiamo,* or *dovete, devono,* or *debbono.*
Future: *dovrò, dovrai, dovrà, etc.*
Subj. pres.: *deva* or *debba, deva* or *debba, deva* or *debba, dobbiamo, dobbiate, devano* or *debbano.*
Cond. pres.: *dovrei, dovresti, dovrebbe, dovremmo, dovreste, etc.*

Fare = to do
Ind. pres.: *fo, fai, fa, facciamo, fate, fanno.*
Imperfect: *facevo, facevi, etc.*
Preterit: *feci, facesti, fece, facemmo, faceste, fecero.*
Subj. pres.: *faccia, etc.*
Subj. imp.: *facessi, etc.*
Imper. pres.: *fa', faccia, etc.*
Past part.: *fatto.*

Godere = to enjoy
Future: *goderò* or *godrò, godrai, godrà, etc.*
Cond. pres.: *godrei, godresti, godrebbe, etc.*

Leggere = to read
Preterit: *lessi, leggesti, lesse, leggemo, leggeste, lessero.*
Past part.: *letto.*

Mettere = to put
Preterit: *misi, mettesti, mise, mettemmo, metteste, misero.*
Past part.: *messo.*

Morire = to die
Ind. pres.: *muoio, muori, muore, moriamo, morite, muoiono.*

Future: *Morirò* or *morrò, etc.*
Subj. pres.: *muoia, etc.*
Cond. pres.: *morirei* or *morrei, etc.*
Pres. part.: *morente.*
Past part.: *morto.*

Nascere = to be born
Preterit: *nacqui, nascesti, nacque, nascemmo,
    nasceste, nacquero.*
Past part.: *nato.*

Nuocere = to hurt, to harm
Ind. pres.: *nuoco, nuoci, nuoce, nociamo, nocete,
    nuocono.*
Preterit: *nocqui, nocesti, nocque, nocemmo,
    noceste, nocquero.*
Subj. pres.: *noccia, noccia, noccia, nocciamo,
    nocciate, nocciano.*
Past part.: *nociuto.*

Piacere = to please, to like
Ind. pres.: *piaccio, piaci, piace, piacciamo, piacete,
    piacciono.*
Preterit: *piacqui, piacesti, piacque, piacemmo,
    piaceste, etc.*
Subj. pres.: *piaccia, etc.*
Past part.: *piaciuto.*

Piovere = to rain
Preterit: *piovve, etc.*
Past part.: *piovuto.*

Potere = to be able
Ind. pres.: *posso, puoi, può, possiamo, potete,
    possono.*

Future: *potrò, potrai, potrà, etc.*
Subj. pres.: *possa, possa, possa, possiamo,
possiate, possano.*
Cond. pres.: *potrei, potresti, potrebbe, etc.*

Ridere = to laugh
Preterit: *risi, ridesti, rise, ridemmo, rideste, risero.*
Past part.: *riso.*

Rimanere = to stay
Ind. pres.: *rimango, rimani, rimane, rimaniamo,
rimanete, rimangono.*
Preterit: *rimasi, rimanesti, rimase, rimanemmo,
rimaneste, rimasero.*
Future: *rimarrò, rimarrai, rimarrà, rimarremo, etc.*
Subj. pres.: *rimanga, etc.*
Cond. pres.: *rimarrei, rimarresti, rimarrebbe, etc.*
Past part.: *rimasto.*

Rispondere = to answer
Preterit: *risposi, rispondesti, rispose, rispondemmo,
rispondeste, risposero.*
Past part.: *risposto.*

Salire = to go up, to climb
Ind. pres.: *salgo, sali, sale, saliamo, salite,
salgono.*
Subj. pres.: *salga, etc.*
Imperative: *sali, salga, saliamo, salite, salgano.*
Past part.: *salito.*

Sapere = to know
Ind. pres.: *so, sai, sa, sappiamo, sapete, sanno.*
Future: *saprò, saprai, saprà, etc.*
Preterit: *seppi, sapesti, seppe, sapemmo, sapeste,
seppero.*
Subj. pres.: *sappia, etc.*
Imperative: *sappi, sappia, etc.*

Cond. pres.: *saprei, sapresti, saprebbe, etc.*
Past part.: *saputo.*

Scegliere = to choose, select
Ind. pres.: *scelgo, scegli, sceglie, scegliamo,*
  scegliete, scelgono.
Preterit: *scelsi, etc.*
Subj. pres.: *scelga, etc.*
Imperative: *scegli, scelga, scegliamo, scegliete,*
  scelgano.
Past part.: *scelto*

Scendere = to go down, descend
Preterit: *scesi, scendeste, scese, scendemmo,*
  scendeste, scesero.
Past part.: *sceso.*

Scrivere = to write
Preterit: *scrissi, scrivesti, scrisse, scrivemmo,*
  scriveste, scrissero.
Past part.: *scritto.*

Sedere = to sit
Ind. pres.: *siedo* or *seggo, siedi, siede, sediamo,*
  sedete, siedono or *seggono.*
Subj. pres.: *sieda* or *segga, etc.*
Imperative: *siedi, sieda* or *segga, etc.*

Stare = to stay; to remain
Ind. pres.: *sto, stai, sta, stiamo, state, stanno.*
Preterit: *stetti, stesti, stette, stemmo, steste, stettero.*
Future: *starò, starai, starà, etc.*
Subj. pres.: *stia, stia, stia, stiamo, stiate, stiano.*
Subj. imper.: *stessi, stessi, stesse, stessimo, steste,*
  stessero.

Imperative: *sta', stia, etc.*
Cond. pres.: *starei, staresti, starebbe, etc.*
Past part.: *stato.*

Tacere = to be silent
Ind. pres.: *taccio, taci, tace, taciamo, tacete, tacciono.*
Preterit: *tacqui, tacesti, tacque, etc.*
Subj. pres.: *taccia, taccia, taccia, taciamo, taciate, tacciano.*
Imperative: *taci, taccia, etc.*
Past part.: *taciuto.*

Udire = to hear, listen
Ind. pres.: *odo, odi, ode, udiamo, udite, odono.*
Future: *udro, udrai, udra, etc.*
Subj. pres.: *oda, etc.*
Condit.: *udirei (udrei).*
Imperative: *odi, oda, udiamo, udite, odano.*

Uscire = to go out
Ind. pres.: *esco, esci, esce, usciamo, uscite, escono.*
Subj. pres.: *esca, etc.*
Imperative: *esci, esca, usciamo, uscite, escano.*

Vedere = to see
Ind. pres.: *vedo* or *veggo, vedi, vede, vediamo, vedete, vedono* or *veggono.*
Preterit: *vidi, videsti, vide, videmmo, videste, videro.*
Future: *vedro, etc.*
Past part.: *veduto* or *visto.*

Venire = to come
Ind. pres.: *vengo, vieni, viene, veniamo, venite, vengono.*
Preterit: *venni, venisti, venne, etc.*
Future: *verrò, verrai, verrà, verremo, etc.*
Subj. pres.: *venga, etc.*
Imperative: *vieni, venga, etc.*
Cond. pres.: *verrei, verresti, verrebbe, etc.*
Pres. part.: *veniente.*
Past part.: *venuto.*

Vivere = to live
Preterit: *vissi, vivesti, visse, vivemmo, viveste, vissero.*
Future: *vivrò, vivrai, vivrà, etc.*
Cond. pres.: *vivrei, vivresti, vivrebbe, etc.*
Past part.: *vissuto.*

Volere = to want
Ind. pres.: *voglio, vuoi, vuole, vogliamo, volete, vogliono.*
Preterit: *volli, volesti, volle, volemmo, voleste, vollero.*
Future: *vorrò, vorrai, vorrà, etc.*
Subj. pres.: *voglia, etc.*
Cond. pres.: *vorrei, vorresti, vorrebbe, etc.*
Past part.: *voluto.*

LETTER WRITING

1. FORMAL INVITATIONS AND ACCEPTANCES

Inviti formali

marzo 1985

Il signore e la signora Peretti hanno il piacere di

annunciare il matrimonio della loro figlia Maria con il signor Giovanni Rossi, ed hanno l'onore di invitare la Signoria Vostra alla cerimonia che avrà luogo nella Chiesa di San Guiseppe, il sei di questo mese, alle ore dodici a.m. Dopo la cerimonia un ricevimento sarà dato in onore degli sposi nella casa dei genitori della sposa.

Mr. and Mrs. Peretti take pleasure in announcing the wedding of their daughter Maria to Mr. John Rossi, and have the honor of inviting you to the ceremony that will take place at the Church of St. Joseph, on the 6th of this month at 12 noon. There will be a reception for the newlyweds afterwards at the residence of the bride's parents.

———————————

Il signore e la signora De Marchi hanno il piacere di invitare il signor Rossi e la sua gentile signora a cena lunedì prossimo, alle otto.

Mr. and Mrs. De Marchi take pleasure in inviting Mr. and Mrs. Rossi to dinner next Monday at 8 o'clock.

———————————

Il signore e la signora Martini hanno il piacere di invitare il signore e la signora Parisi al ricevimento in onore della loro figlia Anna, domenica sera, 19 marzo, alle ore nove.

Mr. and Mrs. Martini take pleasure in inviting Mr. and Mrs. Parisi to a party given in honor of their daughter Anna, on Sunday evening, March 19, at nine o'clock.

—Answers—

Risposte

Il signor Parisi e signora ringraziano per il cortese invito, felici di prendere parte al ricevimento del 19 marzo p.v.

Thank you for your kind invitation. We shall be honored to attend the reception on March 19th.

[Note: *p.v.* = *prossimo venturo,* which means "the next coming" (month). *c.m.* = *corrente mese,* which means "of this month" (the running month.)]

I coniugi Rossi accettano il gentile invito per lunedì prossimo e ringraziano sentitamente.

Mr. and Mrs. Rossi will be honored to have dinner with Mr. and Mrs. De Marchi next Monday. With kindest regards.

I coniugi Rossi ringraziano sentitamente il signore e la signora Peretti per il cortese invito, spiacenti che impegni precedenti non permettano loro di poter accettare.

Mr. and Mrs. Rossi thank Mr. and Mrs. Peretti for their kind invitation and regret that they are unable to come owing to a previous engagement.

2. THANK-YOU NOTE

Roma, 5 marzo 1985

Cara Anna,

Poche righe soltanto per sapere come stai e per ringraziarti del bellissimo vaso che mi hai regalato. L'ho messo sul pianoforte, e ti assicuro che l'effetto è magnifico.

Spero di vederti domani al ricevimento di Angela. Sono sicura che la festa si svolgera con molta allegria.

Mi auguro che latua famiglia stia bene, come posso assicurarti della mia. Ti saluto affettuosamente.

Maria

March 5, 1985

Dear Anna,

This is just to say hello and also to let you know that I received the beautiful vase you sent me as a gift. I've put it on the piano and you can't imagine the beautiful effect.

I hope to see you at Angela's party tomorrow. I think it's going to be a very lively affair.

I hope your family is all well. Everyone here is fine.

Affectionately,

Maria

3. BUSINESS LETTERS

Lettere commerciali

Cavatorta & Co.
Via Veneto 125
Roma—Italia

Ditta Marini e Figli
Via Nomentana 11,
Roma.

Roma, 2 aprile, 1985

Gentili Signori:

Abbiamo il piacere di presentarvi il portatore di questa lettera, signor Carlo Fontanesi, che è uno dei nostri agenti attualmente in vista alle prinicipali città del vostro Paese. Inutile aggiungere che qualsiasi gentilezza sarà usata al signor Fontanesi sarà da noi gradita come un personale favore.

Ringraziandovi in anticipo, vi inviamo i nostri distinti saluti.

Cavatorta & Co.

il Presidente

Cavatorta & Co.
125 Veneto Street
Rome—Italy

(Firm) Marini & Sons
11 Nomentana Street
Rome.

April 2, 1985

Gentlemen:

We have the pleasure of introducing to you the bearer of this letter, Mr. Charles Fontanesi, one of our salesmen, who is visiting the principal cities of your country. Needless to add, we shall greatly appreciate any courtesy you extend to him. (It is needless to say to you that we shall consider any courtesy you extend him as a personal favor.)

Thanking you in advance, we send our best regards.

Cavatorta & Co.

President

_____

Milano, 3 marzo 1985

Signor Giulio Perri
direttore de "Il Mondo"
Via Montenapoleone 3,
Milano.

Gentile Signore:

Includo un assegno di L. 3.000 (tremila), per un anno di abbonamento alla sua rivista.

Distintamente

Lucia Landi

Lucia Landi
Corso Vittorio Emanuele, 8
Roma.

March 3, 1985

Mr. Giulio Perri
Editor of "The World"
3 Montenapoleone Street
Milan.

Dear Sir:

Enclosed please find a check for $5.00 for a year's subscription to your magazine.

Very truly yours,

Lucia Landi

Lucia Landi
8 Corso Vittorio Emanuele
Rome.

4. INFORMAL LETTERS

Caro Giuseppe,

Sono stato molto lieto di ricevere la tua ultima lettera. Prima di tutto desidero darti la grande notizia. Ho finalmente deciso di fare un viaggio fino a Roma, dove intendo rimanere tutto il mese di maggio. Anna verrà con me. Essa è molto felice che avrà così l'occasione di conoscere voi due. La conduco con me perchè essa possa conoscere Roma ed essere di compagnia a tua moglie, ed immagino che insieme avranno l'occasione di pettegolare su ogni cosa, e noi, nel frattempo, potremo trascorrere qualche pomeriggio a nostro agio. Cerca, perciò, di essere possibilmente libero, per allora.

Gli affari vanno bene, e spero che il buon vento continui. L'altro giorno ho visto Antonio, ed egli mi ha chiesto tue notizie.

Ti sarei grato se vorrai riservarci una camera all'albergo Nazionale. Scrivi presto. Saluti ad Elena.

tuo

Giovanni

Dear Joseph,

I was very happy to get your last letter. First of all, let me give you the big news. I have finally decided to make a trip to Rome, where I expect to spend all of May. Anna will come with me. She is extremely happy to be able to meet the two of you at last. I'm bringing her along so that she can see Rome and also so that she can keep your wife company. In this way our wives will have a lot of gossip to share with each other and during this time we will be able to spend some afternoon together at our ease. Try therefore to be as free as you can then.

Business is good now, and I hope will keep that way (that the good wind will continue). I saw Anthony the other day and he asked me about you.

I'd be grateful to you if you would try to reserve a room for us at the "National." Write soon. Give my regards to Helen.

Yours

John

5. FORMS OF SALUTATIONS

Formal

Signore	Sir
Signora	Madam (Mrs.)
Signorina	Miss
Signor Professore	My dear Professor
Eccellentissimo	Your Excellency
Gentile Signor Rossi	My dear Mr. Rossi
Gentile Signora Rossi	My dear Mrs. Rossi
Gentile Signorina Rossi	My dear Miss Rossi

Informal

Caro Antonio	My dear Anthony
Cara Anna	My dear Anna
Mia amata	My beloved
Mio amato	My beloved, my dear
Carissimo Paolo	My very dear Paul
Carissima Giovanna	My very dear Jane

6. FORMS OF COMPLIMENTARY CLOSINGS

Formal

1. *Gradisca i miei piu distinti saluti* (The lei form is used.)

   Very truly yours. (Accept my most distinguished greetings.)

2. *Gradite i miei distinti saluti.* (The voi form is used.)

   Very truly yours. (Accept my distinguished greetings.)

3. *Voglia gradire i miei sinceri saluti.* (The lei form is used.)

   Yours truly. (Accept my sincere greetings.)

4. *Vogliate gradire miei cordiali saluti* (The voi form is used.) — Yours truly. (Accept my heartfelt greetings.)

5. *Devotissimi.* (Can be shortened to Dev. mo.) (The plural form is used.) — Yours truly. (Your very devoted.)

6. *Devotissimo* (Shortened to Dev. mo.) (The singular form is used.) — Yours truly. (Your very devoted.)

Informal

1. *Ricevete i no stri saluti.* — Very sincerely. (Receive our heartfelt greetings.)

2. *In attesa di vostre notizie, vi invio i miei sinceri e cordiali saluti.* — Sincerely yours. (Waiting for your news, I send you my sincere and heartfelt greetings.)

3. *Sperando di ricevere presto tue notizie, t'invio cordialissimi saluti.* — Sincerely yours. (Waiting to hear from you soon, I send you my most heartfelt greetings.)

4. *Tuo amico.* — Sincerely. (Your friend.)

5. *Tua amica.* — Sincerely. (Your friend.)

6. *Affettuosissimo.* (Shortened to Aff.mo) — Affectionately yours. (Very affectionate.)

7. *Affettuosissima.* (Shortened to Aff.ma) — Affectionately yours. (Very affectionate.)

8. *Affezionatissimo.*
   (Aff.mo)

Affectionately yours.
(Very affectionate.)

9. *Non altro, vi invio
   cordiali saluti.*

Sincerely. (No more, I
send you heartfelt
greetings.)

10. *Non altro, t'invio
    cordiali saluti e
    abbracci.*

Sincerely. (No more, I
send you heartfelt
greetings and
embraces.)

11. *Con mille abbracci
    e baci.*

Love. (With a thousand
embraces and kisses.)

12. *Abbracciandoti e
    baciandoti
    caramente.*

Love. (Embracing and
kissing you dearly.)

7. FORM OF THE ENVELOPE

Signor Paolo Bolla
Via Veneto 10
Roma

Spedisce:
Angelo Rossi
Piazza Roma
Napoli

Signora Maria Ferrero
Via Nomentana 27
Roma

Spedisce:
Marcello Marini
Via Montenapoleone
Milano

Signorina Anna Rossi
Piazza Vittorio
    Emanuele 9
Firenze

Spedisce:
Silvana Tarri
Piazza Venezia 71
Roma